SpringerBriefs in Information Systems

Series editor
Jörg Becker

More information about this series at http://www.springer.com/series/10189

Alexander Hütter • René Riedl

Chief Information Officer Role Effectiveness

Literature Review and Implications for Research and Practice

Springer

Alexander Hütter
MIC Customs Solutions
Linz, Austria

René Riedl
University of Applied Sciences Upper Austria
Campus Steyr
Steyr, Austria

Department of Business Informatics —
Information Engineering
University of Linz
Linz, Austria

ISSN 2192-4929   ISSN 2192-4937   (electronic)
SpringerBriefs in Information Systems
ISBN 978-3-319-54752-7   ISBN 978-3-319-54753-4   (eBook)
DOI 10.1007/978-3-319-54753-4

Library of Congress Control Number: 2017937056

Printed on acid-free paper

This Springer imprint is published by Springer Nature
The registered company is Springer International Publishing AG
The registered company address is: Gewerbestrasse 11, 6330 Cham, Switzerland

Contents

Chief Information Officer Role Effectiveness: Literature Review and Implications for Research and Practice

Abstract The effectiveness of the chief information officer (CIO) in organizations is an important topic in the information systems literature because it affects IT success. Recent research is in agreement that an accurate understanding of CIO effectiveness is not possible without considering the organizational roles in which the CIO can operate. Despite the emerging research efforts in this field of study, an integrative perspective on CIO role effectiveness does not exist. To close this research gap, we review the literature in order to develop a set of organizational roles in which the contemporary CIO can act. These CIO roles are termed technology provider, strategic supporter, business thinker, innovation driver, integration advisor, and relationship manager. In consideration of these six CIO roles, we develop a model that comprises four antecedents of role effectiveness, which emerged from analysis of literature on CIO role effectiveness, namely (1) CIO personal competence, (2) CIO hierarchical position, (3) the management environment, and (4) the IT infrastructure of the organization in which the CIO operates. Altogether, our literature review synthesizes the results of highly fragmented work related to CIO role effectiveness reported in 98 studies published during the past three decades. Thereby, we contribute to the information systems literature. First, we integrate what is known about the scope and responsibilities of CIO organizational roles in the present management context. Second, based on our model, we guide research and practice by revealing how and why CIOs can achieve effectiveness in the six roles. Finally, we discuss limitations and potential avenues for future research.

Keywords Chief information officer (CIO) • CIO effectiveness • CIO organizational roles • IT function • IT leadership • IT management • Review • Top management

1 Introduction

The original definition of a chief information officer (CIO) is the "senior executive responsible for establishing corporate information policy, standards, and management control over all corporate information resources" (p. 66) [126]. Over the last 30 years, the contribution of the CIO to organizational success has received

© The Author(s) 2017   1
A. Hütter, R. Riedl, *Chief Information Officer Role Effectiveness*, SpringerBriefs
in Information Systems, DOI 10.1007/978-3-319-54753-4_1

considerable research attention (e.g., [3, 36, 57, 62, 82, 120]). A major conclusion of many studies is that a CIO is essential for multiple reasons. Among others, a CIO can positively influence business performance through strategic information technology (IT) initiatives [93], ensures that investments in IT deliver the expected results [16], and underpins business processes with the appropriate technology [127]. Moreover, evidence shows that shareholders react positively to the announcement of a newly created CIO position [17].

The increasing business dependence on IT has led to fundamental changes in the organizational roles of the CIO over the past decades. In the 1980s, the role of the CIO evolved from operating as a technician (i.e., managing a relatively unimportant service function) to serving as a general manager of an IT department that can influence the success of the entire organization [27, 113]. In the 1990s, the role of the CIO became more powerful. The CIO was often elevated to the level of executive managers, even serving as a member of the top management team (TMT) [2]. As a result, CIOs increasingly focused on strategic issues and began to spend more time interacting with executive and business unit managers outside the IT department [124]. Soon after this rise in importance, however, CIOs began to encounter problems in their efforts to prove value to their chief executive officers (CEOs) and other executive managers. The IT function was frequently perceived as a domain that consumed major resources, but offered little evidence of value [62]. As a consequence, numerous firms decided to outsource their IT function to external service providers [24], and practitioner oriented commentaries on CIOs argued that they were becoming dispensable (e.g., [84]).

Researchers have adopted various approaches to understanding how the organizational role of the CIO evolved, and how CIOs can achieve effectiveness in those roles in order to add value to their firms (for details on related work in this field of study, see Appendix A). Although a number of CIO role descriptions enrich the literature, the wealth of research findings leads to a decrease in manageability of CIO roles in both research and practice. In other words, ambiguity exists regarding the current description of CIO roles, and therefore, an integrative perspective on major individual and organizational antecedents of CIO role effectiveness does not exist. Hence, the objective of this paper is to contribute to the information systems (IS) literature by

- proposing a clear set of CIO roles for the present management context,
- integrating what is known about the antecedents of CIO effectiveness in consideration of the proposed roles (i.e., development of a model), and
- discussing, based on our model, how and why CIOs can achieve effectiveness in the proposed roles.

2   Theoretical Background and Research Gaps

Mintzberg [88, 89] was one of the first scholars who argued that the work of managers can be described in terms of managerial roles. By observing the work activities of managers, he identified ten specific roles that are common to all managerial positions, regardless of their functional or hierarchical level. These ten roles consist of three interpersonal roles (figurehead, leader, and liaison), three informational roles (monitor, disseminator, and spokesperson), and four decisional roles (entrepreneur, disturbance handler, resource allocator, and negotiator). Many other scholars in various academic disciplines replicated, modified, and extended this role classification; generally, their findings confirmed Mintzberg's conceptualization of managerial roles (e.g., [68, 83, 91, 92]).

However, in the early 1980s, approximately one decade after Mintzberg's seminal work, the various innovations in the IT domain led to major challenges in IT leadership within organizations. Thus, it became clear that general executive managers would not be able to successfully manage the IT domain. As a consequence, a new managerial role for the leader of the IT function emerged; the "chief information officer" was born.[1] Importantly, whether or not the ten roles of general management proposed by Mintzberg would also apply to the CIO was not clear during that time. As two of the first IS scholars, Ives and Olson [53] applied Mintzberg's model for investigating the nature of CIOs' work and the related management activities. Based on their findings, Ives and Olson concluded that the new managerial role of the CIO does indeed have idiosyncrasies that cannot be covered based on a general management role model.

More than a decade later, Grover et al. [38] used Mintzberg's model as a framework for examining which managerial role is appropriate for the CIO when IT management matures, and when the centralization of the IT resource increases. Results show that the roles as spokesperson (interacting with the TMT and other areas of organizational management) and liaison officer (establishing external relationships) became more important when IT management matured. Moreover, results indicate that the more centralized the IT resource, the more distinct the CIO's role as spokesperson, monitor (scanning the external environment to keep up with technical changes), and resource allocator (allocating human, financial, and information resources). These initial studies on the organizational roles of the CIO in the 1980s and 1990s motivated further investigations on CIO roles that span the mid-1990s to the present day (for details, see Appendix A).

However, the research on CIO roles and their antecedents of effectiveness in organizations has resulted in separate research conversations and hampering cross-pollination of ideas and findings over the past decades [61]. One major reason for

---

[1]William Synnott is credited with coining the label "chief information officer" in a speech at the 1980 Information Management Exposition and Conference. A few years later, the Business Week magazine titled a story "Management's Newest Star: Meet the Chief Information Officer" to announce the arrival of the CIO (see [8]).

this ambiguity on the CIO roles is that the abstraction level underlying the description of CIO roles varies. The higher the abstraction level, the fewer the number of possible CIO roles. For example, Chen and Wu [18] describe eight different roles, while Leidner and Mackay [73] describe three roles. Another reason for role ambiguity is that the CIO role names are not consistently used in different papers. For example, Smaltz et al. [120] refer to a CIO who mainly focuses on operational IT tasks as "Utility provider", while Li et al. [75] refer to exactly the same role as "IT manager".

Historically, with the increasing organizational focus on technology in strategic business decisions, the responsibilities of the CIO shifted more and more to issues related to IT infrastructure and IT architecture [121]. In order to address these issues in a comprehensive manner, many organizations decided to introduce the role of the chief technology officer (CTO) [87], which further contributed to CIO role ambiguity, or even created confusion. However, a discussion of the roles and responsibilities of the CTO and other CxOs related to the IS function (e.g., chief digital officer, CDO, e.g., [48]) is beyond the scope of this paper.[2]

Due to the ambiguity surrounding the CIO roles, important antecedents of CIO role effectiveness are still not clearly described in the literature. A major reason for this research gap is the sometimes conflicting research findings. An example for such inconsistencies is that papers argue that the CIO reporting structure and the CIO's formal interactions with TMT members are important antecedents of CIO role effectiveness (e.g., [103, 139]). However, other studies indicate that the CIO reporting relationship with the CEO, as well as the extent of the CIO's formal interactions with the CEO and other TMT members, have no significant impact on CIO role effectiveness (e.g. [120]). Such discrepancy in research findings may be the result of varying context (e.g., industry) across different studies or differences in the applied research method (e.g., survey vs. interview). The model of Smaltz et al. [120], for example, was tested in the context of the healthcare industry (which is a highly dynamic, information intensive, and complex industry), and thus special conditions related to CIO role effectiveness may exist in this industry.

Despite these inconsistencies and discrepancies in the literature, there is a clear agreement that an accurate understanding of CIO effectiveness is not possible without considering the organizational roles in which a CIO can act. A major reason for this agreement is rooted in the ever increasing recognition of the advancing IT complexity and the resulting wealth of different responsibilities with which the contemporary CIO has to deal (e.g., [81, 75, 95]).

CIO role ambiguity is a potential reason why CIOs repeatedly underperform in their job, and why firms continue to struggle with the benefits received from their IT portfolio [51, 93, 130]. Hence, we continue by reviewing the literature in order to develop a set of clear CIO roles in the contemporary management context, and to

---

[2]Concerning the CTO, interested readers are referred to the technology management research stream (e.g., see the references in [121]) and the research and development management research stream (e.g., see [144] and the references in [87]).

develop a model that integrates what is known about CIO role effectiveness into the current IS research stream.

3 Literature Review and Model Development

3.1 Methodology

The methodology for identifying literature on CIO role effectiveness proceeded in three steps [135]. First, we queried journal databases on keywords including "chief information officer" and "role" or "effectiveness" (time constraint: 1980–2015).[3] Second, we reviewed the references in the papers identified in the first step to identify additional publications. Finally, we used Web of Science to identify papers citing the papers identified in the previous steps. To evaluate whether an identified paper is concerned with, or relevant to, the topic of CIO role effectiveness, we examined each paper's abstract. This entire process resulted in 98 papers for in-depth review and coding (see Appendix B where we summarize our results based on assignment of papers to publication outlets).[4]

3.2 Conceptualization of the CIO Roles

We reviewed all 98 papers in order to determine whether they contain relevant descriptions of CIO roles. This process resulted in the identification of 48 CIO role descriptions (see the table in Appendix C). To develop a uniform set of CIO roles for the contemporary management context, the first author of this paper analyzed all 48 CIO role descriptions for similarities and differences in order to develop a parsimonious, yet meaningful, set of organizational roles for the contemporary management context. Based on this analysis, the first author conceptualized a set of organizational role categories in which the present CIO can act. Then, the first author mapped all CIO role descriptions identified in the literature to these developed CIO role categories. After completion of the categorization, the second author of this paper reviewed the results in order to identify inappropriate CIO role categories or mappings. At the end of this review process, we discussed the results together, and after some minor modifications and clarifications, we agreed on a final set of six CIO role categories. The roles are termed technology provider, strategic

---

[3]We used the following journal databases: AIS Electronic Library, EBSCOhost, and Science Direct.

[4]In addition to insights on CIO role effectiveness, we also coded each paper's research method, sample size, and country of investigation. We elaborate on these methodological aspects in Appendix E.

supporter, business thinker, innovation driver, integration advisor, and relationship manager. Figure 1 illustrates how the 48 CIO roles from the literature are mapped to our six salient CIO roles. The arrows in Fig. 1 indicate which CIO roles from the literature were used in a more recent paper with a different name (e.g., the "utility provider" by Smaltz et al. [120] served as foundation for the "IT manager" by Li et al. [75]). More details about the categorization process of the six CIO roles are provided in Appendix C.

Table 1 shows the definition of each CIO role, and summarizes how the six roles differ with respect to their responsibilities.

The six developed CIO roles constitute the conceptual foundation for the CIO role effectiveness model in the sections to follow.

3.3 Conceptualization of the CIO Role Effectiveness Model

To conceptualize a model of CIO role effectiveness that shapes and bounds accumulated knowledge, we describe CIO effectiveness based on the six organizational roles of the CIO that we have developed (see Fig. 1 and Table 1). We only include papers in the conceptualization of our model that recognize the importance of examining CIO effectiveness based on multiple roles. This procedure is purposeful to develop insight into CIO effectiveness as a function of different organizational roles. For example, business competence is important for the CIO's job performance in general, but not all CIO roles need business competence to achieve role effectiveness; a technology provider (see Table 1), for instance, can achieve role effectiveness with predominantly technical knowledge [73, 95].

We analyzed all 98 papers in order to identify constructs, as well as relationships among the constructs, which are important for the conceptualization of a CIO role effectiveness model. Thereby, we focused on papers in the conceptualization of our model that recognize the importance of examining CIO effectiveness based on multiple roles. With respect to analysis of papers with the method "survey", we considered only those constructs and relationships that are tested for significance. With respect to analysis of papers with the method "interview" or "conceptual", we take into account the proposed constructs and relationships. This process resulted in a wealth of different constructs. In order to harmonize these constructs, we developed a set of salient CIO role effectiveness constructs. Then, we mapped all constructs identified in the literature to our set of CIO role effectiveness constructs guided by the proposed relationships in the papers. Details about the mapping of the constructs and relationships are provided in the tables in Appendix D.

Figure 2 shows our model of CIO role effectiveness. Based on the literature review, we theorize that four constructs (i.e., CIO personal competence, CIO hierarchical position, management environment, and IT infrastructure) affect CIO role effectiveness. Moreover, Fig. 2 shows that relationships exist among the four constructs. The relationships are supported by our identified literature (see our detailed analysis in Appendix D). Specifically, we theorize that CIO personal

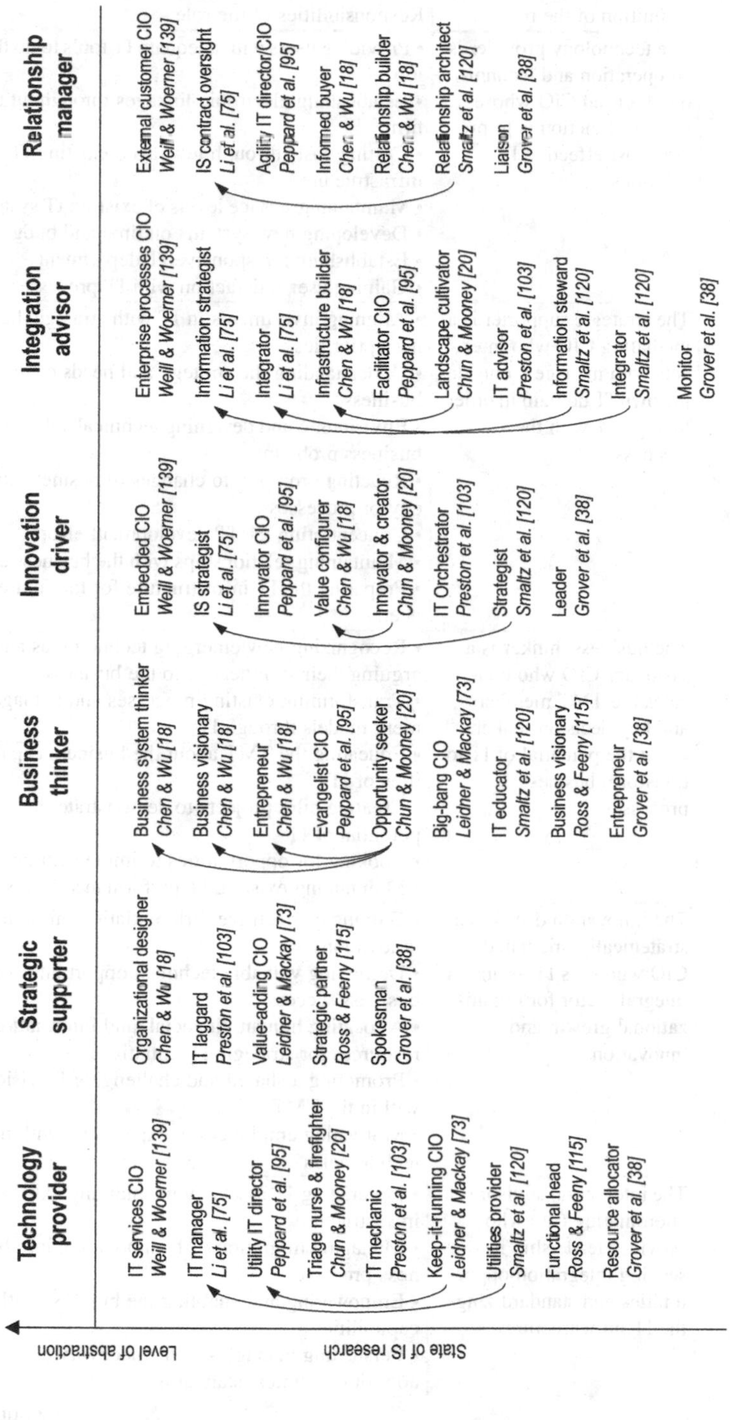

Technology provider	Strategic supporter	Business thinker	Innovation driver	Integration advisor	Relationship manager
IT services CIO Weill & Woerner [139]	Organizational designer Chen & Wu [18]	Business system thinker Chen & Wu [18]	Embedded CIO Weill & Woerner [139]	Enterprise processes CIO Weill & Woerner [139]	External customer CIO Weill & Woerner [139]
IT manager Li et al. [75]	IT laggard Preston et al. [103]	Business visionary Chen & Wu [18]	IS strategist Li et al. [75]	Information strategist Li et al. [75]	IS contract oversight Li et al. [75]
Utility IT director Peppard et al. [95]	Value-adding CIO Leidner & Mackay [73]	Entrepreneur Chen & Wu [18]	Innovator CIO Peppard et al. [95]	Integrator Li et al. [75]	Agility IT director/CIO Peppard et al. [95]
Triage nurse & firefighter Chun & Mooney [20]	Strategic partner Ross & Feeny [115]	Evangelist CIO Peppard et al. [95]	Value configurer Chen & Wu [18]	Infrastructure builder Chen & Wu [18]	Informed buyer Chen & Wu [18]
IT mechanic Preston et al. [103]	Spokesman Grover et al. [38]	Opportunity seeker Chun & Mooney [20]	Innovator & creator Chun & Mooney [20]	Facilitator CIO Peppard et al. [95]	Relationship builder Chen & Wu [18]
Keep-it-running CIO Leidner & Mackay [73]		Big-bang CIO Leidner & Mackay [73]	IT Orchestrator Preston et al. [103]	Landscape cultivator Chun & Mooney [20]	Relationship architect Smaltz et al. [120]
Utilities provider Smaltz et al. [120]		IT educator Smaltz et al. [120]	Strategist Smaltz et al. [120]	IT advisor Preston et al. [103]	Liaison Grover et al. [38]
Functional head Ross & Feeny [115]		Business visionary Ross & Feeny [115]	Leader Grover et al. [38]	Information steward Smaltz et al. [120]	
Resource allocator Grover et al. [38]		Entrepreneur Grover et al. [38]		Integrator Smaltz et al. [120]	
				Monitor Grover et al. [38]	

Level of abstraction

State of IS research

Fig. 1 CIO role model

Table 1 The CIO roles in a contemporary context

CIO role	Definition of the role	Responsibilities of the role
Technology provider	The technology provider is an operation and technology focused CIO whose primary function is to provide cost-effective IT solutions	• Providing users with adequate IT tools to do their job • Establishing electronic linkages throughout the firm • Cutting costs through leveraged existing IT infrastructure • Maintaining service levels of existing IT systems • Developing new systems on time and budget • Establishing a responsive IT department • Gaining user satisfaction with IT processes
Strategic supporter	The strategic supporter is a mediating CIO who interacts with managers outside the own IT domain in order to align IT with the business	• Aligning investments in IT with strategic business priorities • Understanding the strategy and needs of the business • Envisioning and designing technical solutions to business problems • Reacting promptly to changes in business strategy or processes • Concentrating the IT development effort • Maintaining relationships with the business units • Preparing the IT infrastructure for the future needs
Business thinker	The business thinker is a visionary CIO who educates the TMT members and key decision-makers about the potential of IT to transform business processes	• Recognizing new emerging technologies and arguing their significance to the business • Transforming existing processes and management models through IT • Educating the TMT about the business capabilities of IT • Creating pilot projects to demonstrate the potential of IT • Looking for opportunities to implement new IT • Maintaining existing IT performance levels
Innovator driver	The innovation driver is a strategically orientated CIO who uses IT as an integral factor for organizational growth and innovation	• Gaining competitive differentiation through IT innovations • Delivering valuable technical opportunities for business success • Allocating human, financial, and information resources for strategic IT initiatives • Promoting a shared and challenging IT vision within the TMT • Motivating employees to experiment with new technologies
Integration advisor	The integration advisor is a coordinating CIO who provides leadership in seeking integration opportunities and standardizing the IT infrastructure	• Leveraging IT assets by maintaining existing IT infrastructure • Managing migration of IT innovation into business processes • Empowering and enabling the business with IT capabilities • Persuading managers of the necessity of adopting technical standards

(continued)

Table 1 (continued)

CIO role	Definition of the role	Responsibilities of the role
		• Analyzing the external environment to keep up with technical changes • Providing valuable information for decision-making (big data issues)
Relationship manager	The relationship manager is a bridge-building CIO who communicates with the external environment in order to meet a distinct set of IT requirements	• Exchanging information with suppliers, customers, buyers, and market analysts • Selecting a sourcing strategy to meet business needs and technological issues • Coordinating the organizational IT requirements • Setting technical standards and policies • Scanning the developing IT services market • Developing an agile IT infrastructure • Guaranteeing security and privacy

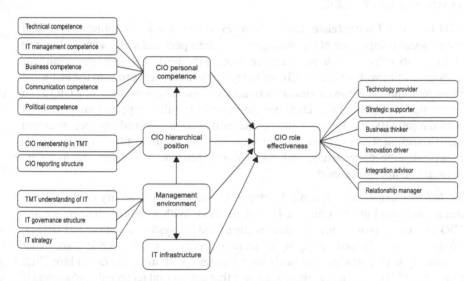

Fig. 2 Model of CIO role effectiveness

competence directly affects CIO role effectiveness. Further, CIO hierarchical position exerts direct influence on CIO role effectiveness, but also determines the required CIO personal competencies for this position. The management environment in which a CIO operates has a direct impact on CIO role effectiveness, and also an indirect impact (mediation via CIO hierarchical position and IT infrastructure). Finally, the IT infrastructure also directly influences CIO role effectiveness.

CIO personal competence has five dimensions (technical competence, IT management competence, business competence, communication competence, and political competence). CIO hierarchical position within the organization has two dimensions (CIO membership in the TMT and the CIO reporting structure). The management environment in which the CIO operates has three dimensions (TMT understanding of IT, IT governance structure, and IT strategy). The final construct is the IT infrastructure of an organization in which the CIO operates. Next, we define the model and the underlying mechanisms in detail, and do so with explicit consideration of the six CIO organizational roles.

CIO Role Effectiveness CIO role effectiveness is defined as "the assessed performance of the CIO in the context of specific roles, behaviors, and responsibilities that are regarded as salient in firms" (p. 208) [120]. Organizational behavior and human resource management literature argue that if employees enact multiple roles beyond that of jobholder, those roles that are considered important from an organizational perspective should be measured through a comprehensive assessment of employee performance (e.g., [14, 129, 140]). To assess CIO role effectiveness, the common approach in IS research is to measure the extent to which CIOs fulfill their business peers' expectations regarding the responsibilities that are associated with a specific role [18, 75, 120].

CIO Personal Competence Research in several academic disciplines has related the personal competence of top managers (i.e., their personal skills, knowledge, and abilities) to effective job performance (e.g., [45, 86]). Through the wealth of responsibilities with which the CIO of today has to deal (in contrast to the historical focus on technical issues), IS research treats the personal competence of a CIO as an emerging antecedent of role effectiveness in order to fulfill expectations associated with the job [10, 18]. Personal competencies that have received research attention include technical competence, IT management competence, business competence, communication competence, and political competence. We detail the five CIO personal competencies next.

Technical Competence Technical competence refers to the ability of the CIO to design and develop cost-effective IT systems [97]. With technical competence, the CIO possesses proficiency in infrastructure design, system analysis and design, programming [85], and setting up of technical contracts [35]. While some older studies argue that management skills are becoming predominantly critical for CIOs (e.g., [82, 113]), more recent papers suggest that a profound technical background is important for CIOs to succeed in their job [69, 122]. Through technical competence, CIOs are better able to construct sophisticated IT systems and applications, and to connect different business functional units in a value chain [116].

IT Management Competence IT management competence refers to the ability of the CIO to manage strategic IT projects, evaluate technology options, and assist the TMT with IT investment decisions [3, 21]. Researchers also refer to this competence as supply-side leadership (e.g., [19]). Managerial IT competence enhances a CIO's ability to envision and produce technical solutions to important business problems [97]. Such a strategic orientation toward the business leads to IT-business alignment and improved business performance [15]. Also, the IT management competence of the CIO reduces the costs and lead times of IT development processes [33].

Business Competence Business competence refers to the ability of the CIO to understand an organization's business strategies, priorities, opportunities, and needs for the strategic and innovative use of IT [21, 75]. Researchers also refer to this competence as demand-side leadership (e.g., [19]). With business competence, CIOs are better able to understand an organization's processes, products and services, industry conditions for success, and competitors' strength and weaknesses [3]. Such a broad business perspective enables CIOs to make appropriate decisions about IT and business investments, match new market opportunities with technology, and support innovation for growth [18, 134]. It also facilitates the development of a shared understanding between the CIO and TMT members regarding the role of IT in the organization [102].

Communication Competence Communication competence is defined as the ability of the CIO to "communicate clearly, persuasively, and in business terms" (p. 211) [120]. A major responsibility of CIOs is to provide base IT services to all organizational units; thus, CIOs must be adept at educating other departments with varied backgrounds and motivations to use IT to support business processes, and to motivate other people to experiment with new technologies [101, 109]. Hence, the challenge for CIOs is to explain IT issues in terminology that is understood by others who are not familiar with the technology. CIOs who are proficient in speaking in business terms are more effective in creating a shared vision than are those who use technical language or frame the issues in terms of technical implications [36, 101]. However, business executives have complained that their CIOs sometimes lack the ability to speak in "business language". This can hinder the ability of the CIO to work effectively with the TMT on strategic objectives [128].

Political Competence Political competence is defined as the ability of the CIO to influence business executives to commit to strategic IT initiatives, persuade them to participate in the initiatives, and negotiate the appropriate resources [31, 120]. CIOs are commonly faced with promoting and managing technological changes for which the focus is often in functional areas outside of their direct control. Skill in exercising influence can be a major contributor to the CIO's success in gaining peer commitment [31]. Implementing technological changes typically requires collaboration across departmental boundaries within an organization. Thus, networking with top executives and key decision makers is important for CIOs in order to be able to establish collaborations and trusting relationships [109, 134]. Only through these trusting relationships can CIOs ensure that both business and technology capabilities are integrated into effective IT solutions [114].

CIO Hierarchical Position In general, the organizational position of an individual provides a legitimate base for influencing organizational actions and decisions [4, 30]. The IS literature examines the importance of CIO hierarchical position to develop impact on organizational actions and decisions. A major theory that has guided much of this research stream is the upper echelons theory [41, 42]. The upper echelons theory emphasizes that the characteristics of top managers, as well as the nature of their interactions and exchanges, are important factors influencing strategic decisions and resulting business outcomes. Hence, CIO hierarchical position is another construct that may affect CIO role effectiveness. This construct has two dimensions: CIO membership in the TMT and CIO reporting structure.

CIO Membership in the TMT CIO membership in the TMT is defined as the formal or informal involvement of the CIO in top management agendas. Formal involvement means that the CIO has a seat on the table at the management board, which increases CIO authority and power within the organization [41, 120]. Informal involvement means that the CIO is not an official member of the TMT, but has the opportunity for engagements with top managers and is invited to participate in TMT meetings. Higher levels of engagements between the CIO and TMT members are likely to provide the CIO with a greater understanding of the firm's business practices, goals, and vision [3]. These engagements also offer a potential forum for executive managers to better understand the role of IT in supporting the business strategy [28, 102]. Finally, due to membership in the TMT the CIO can derive desired organizational outcomes such as IT-business strategic alignment [64, 114] and higher financial firm performance [107].

CIO Reporting Structure CIO reporting structure is defined as the line that determines to which top manager the CIO reports. A reporting structure is an important decision that a firm must make, because an inappropriate reporting structure impedes a CIO's work [5]. Previous research suggests that the CIO should always report directly to the CEO in order to promote the importance of IT, and to strengthen the CIO's influence in the organization [2, 104, 132]. Reporting to the CFO (chief financial officer), in contrast to reporting to the CEO, has long been considered to signify a diminished role of a CIO because the CIO-CFO reporting structure has been selected, often, as a means of monitoring IT spending. However, recent evidence challenges this notion by arguing that a firm's strategic positioning (differentiation or cost leadership) should be the primary determinant of the CIO reporting structure, irrespective of IT intensity or the role of IT within the organization [5]. As a rule of thumb, differentiators should prefer a CIO-CEO reporting structure, while cost leaders should prefer a CIO-CFO reporting structure [5].

Management Environment of the CIO The management environment of an organization in which the CIO operates is another antecedent of CIO role effectiveness, which has three dimensions: the extent of TMT members' understanding of IT, the IT governance structure, and the IT strategy. We included these dimensions in our theoretical model because they are important factors for determining the nature of the CIO organizational roles [20], and for leveraging a CIO's influence on business outcomes [93].

TMT Understanding of IT TMT understanding of IT refers to the knowledge of business executives of how IT generates value and how IT can be used to support business objectives [6]. Hence, IT understanding of the TMT concerns knowledge on how IT can affect organizational performance, both operationally and strategically [93]. Having IT-competent business executives is important for the success of championing IT within organizations [6, 29]. However, a common problem encountered by CIOs is that business executives often misunderstand the capabilities of IT. Some executives overestimate IT capabilities, while others are unaware of how IT can be used to support business objectives [60, 101]. Such a lack of understanding is problematic for both the CIO and the TMT in order to achieve a shared IT vision [102] and an innovative IT climate [134].

IT Governance Structure IT governance is defined as the structure that specifies decision rights and accountability for important IT decisions [136, 138]. Specifically, IT governance determines who makes which type of decisions, who provides input related to a decision, and how individuals are held accountable for their decisions [17, 136]. IT governance is critical for organizations, because the involvement of business executives in IT decision-making and value-creating processes may significantly affect the value received by IT investments [117, 141]. Effective IT governance encourages business executives to share the risk and accept the responsibility for the strategic thinking around IT deployment and use, and enables CIOs to weave together business and IT strategies [10, 20]. Working in partnership with the CIO in decision-making processes establishes realistic expectations of IT across the TMT and promotes clarification of the business strategy [95].

IT Strategy IT strategy is defined as the formulated, shared, and aspired approach of how IT should support the business. The IT strategy of an organization can be considered as either forward thinking, encouraging innovative approaches of IT to support long-term goals, or as risk-averse, emphasizing rigid support of operations [20, 58, 127]. Organizations with a forward thinking IT strategy view IT as a tool for enhancing and forming business strategies; they invest in IT in order to achieve an IT infrastructure that makes competitive differentiation possible [19, 137]. Organizations with a risk-averse strategy view IT as a utility for providing fundamental IT services at a minimum cost; they invest in IT in order to enhance the quality of IT services or to reduce IT costs [19, 137]. However, if the CIO leadership approach is in conflict with the IT strategy, the CIO role performance may be adversely affected [122], and the organization may struggle to achieve superior performance through IT initiatives [67].

IT Infrastructure IT infrastructure is defined as the shared foundation of IT capability (including both technical and human assets) across the organization in the form of reliable services [13]. If the connectivity of the IT infrastructure and the scope of services that it can support increase, the resources made available by the infrastructure and its ability to support strategic IT initiatives also increase [12, 66]. Furthermore, the IT infrastructure provides the basis for building profitable business applications [114], for assimilating IT into business activities [3], and for enabling IT innovation [26]. However, to achieve a business-driven infrastructure, it has been recommended that business and IT executives should work together and share the responsibility for developing this infrastructure [122]. By the type of IT infrastructure, we distinguish between an integrated infrastructure that is characterized by systematically implemented IT systems across business

processes and organizational units, and an isolated infrastructure that is characterized by many non-standard IT applications, processes, and functions [20].

4 Discussion

Our model (Fig. 2) serves as a lens through which we interpret the findings of more
than three decades of research on CIO role effectiveness. In the following sections,
we discuss how and why CIOs can achieve effectiveness in their different organizational roles.

4.1 *Effectiveness as a Technology Provider*

A technology provider is focused on delivering reliable and cost-efficient IT
services. Thus, this CIO needs profound technical competence in order to establish
electronic linkages throughout the firm and to provide users with adequate IT tools
to do their job [120]. However, the importance of technical competence for CIOs is
discussed controversially in the IS literature. Some papers argue that the growing
complexities of IT infrastructures and IT markets lead to an increased demand for a
CIO with a strong technical background [47, 122]. Other papers argue that managerial IT skills rather than technical skills are crucial for the CIO to achieve
effectiveness because technical issues can be delegated to technical staff or con-
tractors [18, 85].

We believe that this disagreement in the literature has its root cause in the fact
that research often does not consider that CIO effectiveness depends on the role in
which the CIO acts. Considering the set of six CIO roles (Fig. 1 and Table 1),
neither research stream need necessarily be wrong. For example, for a business
thinker who is responsible for shaping the business vision through IT and improving
business process inside and outside a firm, business competence is critical to
achieving role effectiveness, while technical competence is hardly important [95].

A technology provider typically reports to the CFO because the focus of this role
is on cost containment. Reporting to the CFO, in contrast to reporting to the CEO,
has long been considered in the IS literature to signify a diminished role for a CIO,
because the CIO-CFO reporting structure, traditionally, has been selected as a
means of monitoring IT spending. Earlier studies frequently call for a CIO-CEO
reporting structure in order to promote the importance of IT and to strengthen the
CIO's influence on strategic decisions within the organization [2, 37]. Further, with
respect to reporting level, papers often argue that when the CIO is distant from the
CEO this is an indication that the organization does not place high value on IT
[104, 132]. However, more recent studies challenge this notion by arguing that no
CIO reporting structure is necessarily optimal, and that the reporting line should not
be used to determine the role of IT within the organization. Drawing on Porter's

[98, 99] generic business strategies, Banker et al. [5] argue that a firm's strategic positioning (differentiation or cost leadership) should be the primary determinant of the CIO reporting structure. This means that if an organization follows a cost leadership strategy (i.e., implementation of IT systems to reduce organizational costs), a CIO-CFO reporting structure is recommended in order to identify smart opportunities for cost savings. From this perspective, a CIO-CFO reporting structure is adequate to a technology provider.

Organizations with a technology provider are most likely not strategically dependent on IT (or have chosen not to be); they use IT to support operational processes in an efficient and rational manner [95]. Hence, membership in the TMT is not necessary for a technology provider because most interactions of the CIO are with operational staff. The TMT members associate IT primarily with data processing and do not consider that IT can offer additional value for the business [103]. Those top managers often decide to use IT as a utility for providing fundamental IT services at a minimum cost [139]. Consequently, IT is not part of the business strategy and the technology provider has to ensure that the IT portfolio solely meets the agreed service levels and satisfaction of the user community [115], while paying less attention to envisioning major new systems [73]. Due to this risk-averse strategy, the IT infrastructure is characterized by various isolated IT systems and a diverse set of business and operations processes.

4.2 Effectiveness as a Strategic Supporter

The strategic supporter operates in a rather risk-averse IT environment where the systems, applications, and processes are isolated and not targeted to important business objectives [73]. Therefore, a major concern of the strategic supporter is the alignment between an organization's IT objectives and business objectives. Solid IT management competence as well as a basic understanding of the business are required for the strategic supporter in order to match new market opportunities with the appropriate technology, align investments in IT with strategic business priorities, and support organizational business changes for strategic growth [19, 103]. To achieve a partnership with the business, the strategic partner has to cross departmental boundaries and become involved in affairs of other organizational areas outside the IT domain [38]. Communication competence is valuable for the strategic partner in order to connect the IT department to the top level of the organization and to key decision-makers of other business units [18, 133].

The TMT members of the organization in which the strategic partner operates have often heard about the IT success stories in other firms, but they do not know how they could apply IT for their business [73]. To provide TMT members with insights into the capabilities of and opportunities provided by IT, the strategic supporter may report to the CEO. Due to direct access to the CEO (formally defined through a CIO-CEO reporting structure), the CIO can also gain a higher level of understanding of the business, and have access to a great deal of information that is important for the successful exploitation of IT [51, 101]. As a consequence, the strategic supporter is more likely to develop new systems or enhance existing systems that address immediate business needs and also support ongoing business needs [115].

Higher levels of shared cognition between business and IT executives can lead to higher levels of business-IT alignment [128]. When business executives, in particular the CEO, become more knowledgeable about IT opportunities within the firm, the role of IT is more likely to be made explicit in business strategies [49, 64]. The TMT's IT knowledge also has major effects on strategic alignment through planning behaviors and subsequent effects of IT projects on business performance [65, 90]. However, business executives do not necessarily need detailed technical knowledge; rather, they can provide adequate guidance by understanding the basic concepts of IT [3, 29].

Usually, the organization's IT department is responsible for creating and managing the IT infrastructure [96]. In order to create an infrastructure that enables organizations to develop digital agility, CIOs need to translate a firm's strategic intent into appropriate IT investments in a timely manner [114, 118]. CIOs who operate in the strategic supporter role are frequently confronted with limited resources, especially during an economic decline, and organizations often decide to reduce their IT investments to save money [74]. While reducing IT investments might cut costs, future growth hinges on continued IT investments. Thus, those CIOs have to decide carefully how to support new application development for achieving homogeneous IT systems while cutting costs.

4.3   Effectiveness as a Business Thinker

One of the biggest challenges requiring much of business thinkers' time is working on a shared IT understanding among the TMT in order to improve business processes and to take advantage of technological opportunities [20, 115]. However, a frequently encountered problem among business thinkers is that their business executives often misunderstand the capabilities of IT. On the one hand, some business executives do not understand how IT can be used to support business objectives and therefore think that IT is an administrative expense that should be minimized [101, 110]. On the other hand, other business executives overestimate the capabilities of IT and are disappointed when IT does not provide the expected strategic opportunities [6, 67].

These misunderstandings about the capabilities of IT might negatively affect CIOs' strategic management of IT [60], and the level of engagement and involvement of business executives in IT issues and decisions [28, 94]. Hence, both business competence and communication competence are necessary for the business thinker in order to be able to educate the top managers about the potential of IT, and specifically, to manage their expectations of IT [93, 125]. Through business competence, the business thinkers can provide value-added IT perspectives to their top managers and are therefore more likely to positively influence a firm's ability to assimilate IT into its value-chain activities and business strategies [3, 9]. Frequent communication between the CIO and the CEO enables consensus building, reduction of barriers, and achievement of convergence about the role of IT for the business [55, 56, 111]. By communicating and coordinating extensively, the business executives share the risk and accept the responsibility for strategic IT projects, and the business thinker CIO is better able to anticipate business needs and devise appropriate solutions [35, 116].

In order to be an effective educator about the value IT can deliver, the business thinker needs access to those business executives who are responsible for the strategic planning and decision making processes (formal membership in the TMT or a CIO-CEO reporting structure can provide the CIO with appropriate access to business executives) [102, 119]. CIOs who attend TMT meetings gain a higher level of understanding of the business, and have access to a great deal of information that is important for transforming business processes through IT [28, 71, 120]. From the perspective of the TMT, regular meetings with the CIO enable senior management to share ideas and develop a better understanding of the strategic business and IT issues surrounding IT assimilation [3, 21]. The more the TMT is familiar with IT, the more likely it is that the CIO will be able to negotiate expectations in an informed and rational manner, and meet those expectations [95].

Organizations with a business thinker CIO have often set up their technological environment according to their technical needs, but there are plenty of opportunities to improve business processes, and to exploit strategic opportunities. Hence, the challenge for a business thinker is to convince TMT members to maintain and transform existing processes, products, and management models through IT [20]. Thus, political competence is critical for the business thinker in order to gain business executives' commitment to strategic IT projects [31]; also, IT competence is important for leading those projects [134].

4.4 Effectiveness as an Innovation Driver

The innovation driver is mainly concerned with higher revenue generation and achieving competitive differentiation through IT innovations. Due to the fundamental strategic orientation toward the business, the innovation driver needs a comprehensive understanding of the business to be able to deliver meaningful technical or business innovations [95, 139]. Business competence is also the key for the innovation driver in the development of a shared vision of the role of IT within the organization [100], which, in turn, can leverage TMT support for the successful planning and implementation of strategic IT initiatives [125].

To make innovation possible, the TMT members of the organization in which the innovation driver operates must understand and agree that IT is a key contributor to the business, and there must also be willingness of employees to experiment with new technologies [75, 103]. Furthermore, the TMT members have to decide to follow a forward-thinking IT strategy (i.e., use IT as a tool for gaining competitive differentiation through IT innovations), and to integrate its IT systems across the organization to enable the development and implementation of process innovations [20]. On the other hand, effective demand-side leadership by the CIO is critical for creating new strategic growth and competitive differentiation through IT investments [19], and for demonstrating that each IT project contributes to forming the business outcomes [11].

To drive the organization forward in the use of IT, the innovation driver is called on to take part as a formal or at least an informal member of the TMT board. Attendance at executive meetings provides the innovation driver with better opportunities for addressing an organization's strategic IT management and use challenges [60, 120]. Research indicates that firms that accord a higher status to their CIOs and include them in the TMT can exhibit better financial performance [107]. Conversely, the greater the distance between the CEO and the CIO, the poorer the impact of IT investments on the financial performance of firms [62, 76].

Following Banker et al.'s [5] notion that a firm's strategic positioning (differentiation or cost leadership) should be the primary determinant of the CIO reporting structure, the innovation driver should report directly to the CEO in order to achieve competitive differentiation through strategic IT initiatives. An innovation driver can benefit from reporting to the CEO in order to allocate the human, financial, and information resources that are necessary for implementing strategic IT initiatives. Exploring the aspects of developing a shared CIO/TMT understanding regarding the role of IT, Preston and Karahanna [101] argue that when the CIO reports to the CEO, the CIO and the TMT are more likely to reach a congruent IT vision.

To establish a strategically relevant IT system (e.g., an ERP system) or IT process within the organization, the innovation driver has to successfully exert influence in order to provide business support for technological changes, and negotiate the required resources for the strategic initiative [32, 72, 120]. Thus, political competence is required for the innovation driver to achieve role effectiveness. Specific influence behaviors (i.e., rational persuasion and personal appeal) can be key contributors to the success of the CIO in gaining peer commitment, while the use of other behaviors (e.g., pressure) may lead to peer resistance [31]. CIOs who have the ability to influence and persuade others are more effective in pioneering the exploitation of IT in new tasks and settings with the aim toward improving products and services or enhancing organizational efficiency and effectiveness [78].

An effective IT governance structure is important to the innovation driver CIO because it defines how coordination across businesses and functions is achieved, how IT resources are allocated and risk is managed, and how oversight is provided [80, 136]. Hunter [51] provides evidence for a scenario in which the CIO introduces a strong IT governance structure with the active support of the CEO. With the support of the CEO, the CIO pushed responsibility for many aspects of IT out to colleagues in the business domain. There was a strong business involvement in all IT-enabled change projects (there were no IT projects) and no IT investment went ahead without strong business sponsorship. Due to this involvement of business executives in IT-related decisions, such as developing strategy and investment prioritization, the CIO achieved superior role performance. A similar effect was also found in prior studies, suggesting that executive involvement is more strongly associated with the firm's progressive use of IT than executive participation in IT activities [54, 105]. This involvement also positively influences the TMT's support for strategic IT initiatives [25, 63].

4.5 Effectiveness as an Integration Advisor

The integration advisor is focused on leveraging IT assets by exploiting the existing IT resources. Therefore, IT management competence is essential for the integration advisor to gain value from IT exploitation without disrupting the business strategy [20]. A fundamental understanding of the business is also compulsory for the integration advisor in order to be able to provide leadership in seeking integration opportunities and ensure that the IT infrastructure is fully embedded into the organization [77, 120]. Especially when business executives take ownership of the strategic exploitation of IT, the integration advisor has to underpin their initiatives with the appropriate technology, and has to assure compliance with the corporate IT strategy [95].

The organizations in which an integration advisor operates are often heavily dependent on their IT infrastructure in accomplishing their daily business activities [75]. To develop an IT infrastructure that meets ongoing known business needs, the integration advisor must work together with various organizational areas to gather the required information for decision-making [58]. Especially when an integration advisor has to deal with an inappropriate IT infrastructure (e.g., various legacy systems), frequent communication with the organizational areas using this infrastructure is important for developing a concept to renew the existing IT systems [21]. Due to effective communication, the CIO can also provide key decision-makers with an appropriate perspective on how to align existing IT resources with organizational strategies and structures [22, 80, 108].

Integrated IT systems and applications across business processes and organizational units provide a solid foundation for integration advisors to add value to their organizations, and enable firms to react more quickly to changes in the competitive environment [28, 103]. The sophistication of an IT infrastructure also significantly influences firms' ability to utilize IT in their value-chain activities and business strategies [3]. Creating systematic business processes and leveraging IT assets throughout the organization is difficult when the CIO has to deal with many non-standard IT applications, processes, and functions. In that case, the advice for the CIO is to work on stabilizing the IT applications and processes and on providing cost savings by better integrating the IT systems, and then educating all employees on technology initiatives that will change the current situation [20].

However, in general, the integration advisor is accepted by the TMT as a trusted partner, and may participate as formal member, or at least as informal member, in the TMT. In addition, the integration advisor may report to the CEO. Due to this structural involvement in the organization's TMT, the integration advisor has access to a great deal of information that is important for the successful exploitation of IT [28, 71, 120]. When the integration advisor participates in TMT meetings, the business executives can also gain insights into technological perspectives, and therefore are better able to uncover potential ways to further leverage IT as a core competence [54, 65]. As a consequence, business executives are more likely to be participating in the governance of IT, because they understand that strategic opportunities provided by IT cannot be fully exploited without support from the business side [51, 139].

4.6 Effectiveness as a Relationship Manager

A relationship manager is focused on networking with the external environment including the exchange of information with suppliers, customers, buyers, and market analysts in order to meet a distinct set of IT requirements [139]. Based on these requirements, the relationship manager defines appropriate IT contracts, monitors those contracts in terms of agreed service levels and financial scope, and maintains information policies and standards [75]. Further, a relationship manager assures security and privacy of the IT environment, and is also responsible for risk management [120]. Thus, it is important for a CIO in this role to establish effective relationships with external partners, including an extensive network of technology suppliers [18]. In order to accomplish these tasks, the relationship manager needs profound IT management competence and communication competence, as well as extensive knowledge of the organization's business processes and priorities.

Relationship managers who achieve both appropriateness and effectiveness in their social interactions can improve their relationships with both internal and external parties [109, 123]. Those relationships are important for the CIO to implement technological changes within an organization because these changes typically require collaborations across departmental boundaries [59, 142]. In a valuable relationship, IT and business functional units work together to better understand business opportunities, determine needed functionality, choose among technology options, and share the risk and responsibility for the effective application of IT within the organization [116, 134]. Trusting relationships with key executives also enable CIOs to facilitate mutual cooperation and participation in strategy development, which lead to greater alignment between IT and business priorities [79, 128], and leverage the successful utilization of IT resources for superior performance [40, 70].

The business executives of the organization in which the relationship manager operates principally understand the potential strategic and operational role of IT, but they need an individual who can match their aspirations with advanced knowledge from the technology supply side [23]. Therefore, the implementation of an IT governance structure within the organization, or the implementation of regular IT steering committees where the business executives participate, provides a possibility for the CIO to advise them on technological capabilities, policies, and risks [139]. Also, relationship managers can use this organizational structure to keep their business executives up with technological changes and competition that may affect their own IT environment [38].

A relationship manager can principally operate under a risk-averse IT strategy, but a forward-thinking IT strategy makes their daily work effective. By a risk-averse strategy, the relationship manager has to concentrate on the cost and quality of IT services [11]. Thus, it would be advisable for the relationship manager to show that each IT project provides clear cost savings and/or quality enhancements, if compared to existing IT services. If the IT function struggles with providing cost-effective and reliable services to the business, developing effective supply-side leadership by the CIO is compulsory [19].

5 Implications

5.1 Research Implications

Compatibility of the CIO Roles: A Proposal In this paper, we show that an accurate understanding of CIO effectiveness is not possible without consideration of the organizational roles in which contemporary CIOs operate (i.e., technology provider, strategic supporter, business thinker, innovator driver, integration advisor, or relationship manager). The complexity and wealth of responsibilities with which the contemporary CIO has to deal are steadily increasing in today's digital economy. Thus, without considering the CIO's work in the context of multiple roles, the present CIO may not be able to champion all responsibilities that are associated with effectiveness [139]. Consequently, research should place emphasis on examining CIO effectiveness as a function of multiple roles.

Due to the wealth of responsibilities with which the CIO of today has to deal (see Table 1), CIOs are increasingly called upon to be effective in multiple roles. However, the compatibility of different CIO roles is not well understood today; yet, the importance of this compatibility for achieving role effectiveness has already been made the subject of discussion in the CIO literature [60]. By comparing the CIO responsibilities that are associated with the six roles (Table 1), it becomes evident that it is hardly possible for a CIO to fulfill all responsibilities of all roles at the same time. Figure 3 summarizes our proposal about which CIO roles may fit together, and which CIO roles are not, or less, compatible in our opinion.

We argue that the roles of technology provider and strategic supporter may be compatible with each other because joint consideration of both roles is more likely to be able to provide users with IT solutions that are aligned with the business at a minimum cost. With respect to the CIO's hierarchical position, however, it is necessary to analyze whether a strategic supporter can operate effectively with a CIO-CFO reporting structure. Moreover, the roles of technology provider and

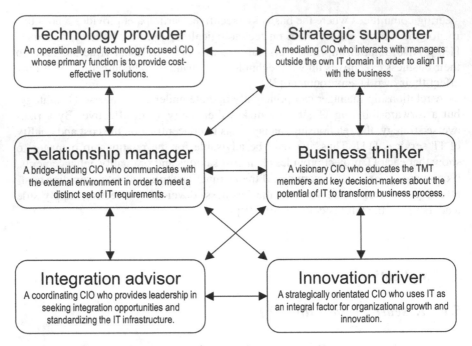

Fig. 3 Compatibility of the CIO roles

relationship manager may also be mutually compatible because the CIO who operates in these roles coordinates the organizational IT requirements through interaction with service providers, and is thus more likely able to develop new systems on time and within budget. The roles of technology provider and business thinker are mutually exclusive because when the CIO has no access to the TMT, it is hardly possible to educate the top managers about the IT capabilities and to build a shared IT vision. Similarly, technology provider and innovation driver are mutually exclusive roles because when the TMT does not believe in the business value of IT, it is hardly possible for the CIO to deliver meaningful technical or business innovations. Furthermore, without access to the TMT as technology provider (due to a missing CIO-CEO reporting structure), it is hardly possible for the integration advisor to successfully manage transformation of IT innovations into efficient business processes. Hence, the roles of technology provider and integration advisor are hardly compatible.

The strategic supporter and the business thinker may fit together because CIOs who operate in these roles frequently interact with managers outside the IT domain, and can thereby positively influence their mindsets about IT. Also, the strategic supporter and the relationship manager may fit together as effective communication is a major success factor of both roles. However, the CIO roles of strategic supporter and innovation driver, as well as integration advisor, are mutually exclusive because the strategic supporter does not have the necessary organizational power (no membership in the TMT) to ensure continued investment in strategic IT opportunities (as the innovation driver) and to empower the business with IT capabilities (as the integration advisor).

The roles of business thinker and innovation driver, as well as that of integration advisor, may fit together because the improvement of business processes (business thinker), implementation of new strategic IT systems across the corporation based on these process improvements (innovation driver), and finally, management of the integration of the strategic IT systems into a standardized IT infrastructure (integration adviser) are logically successive and hence related activities. Moreover, the business thinker and relationship manager may also fit together because the CIOs who operate in these roles frequently exchange information with internal and external parties (e.g., suppliers, customers, and service providers), and thereby recognize new emerging technologies and then argue their significance for the business.

The roles of innovation driver and integration advisor may fit together because the CIOs who operate in these roles promote a shared and challenging understanding of IT within the TMT, and thereby are forward-thinking about technological changes. Both roles possess the necessary organizational power to accomplish this task. Additionally, the roles of innovation driver and relationship manager may fit together because in both roles the CIO can allocate the human, financial, and information resources for strategic IT initiatives, while simultaneously having a focus on the goal that IT contracts remain within scope and budget. Finally, the integration advisor and the relationship manager may fit together because the CIO who operates in these roles regularly scans the IT market, thereby collecting useful information for decision-making.

The development of our proposal is based on conceptual arguments. Thereby, note that perceived correctness of our compatibility classification in Fig. 3 is affected by (1) agreement on the major characteristics of each CIO role (see Table 1) and (2) agreement on whether the characteristics of two roles are in conflict or not. While it is less likely that disagreement exists with respect to point (1), disagreement is more likely regarding point (2). Thus, we see our classification in Fig. 3 as a starting point, one that should instigate future research. Foremost, a survey with CIOs as informants is encouraged to assess the compatibility of the six roles from their perspective.

Measuring CIO Role Effectiveness The related work on CIO role effectiveness (see Appendix A) evaluates this construct based on business executives' assessment of the extent to which a CIO fulfills the expectations that are associated with a specific role. This approach is not without limitations because sometimes a mismatch exists between how CIOs and business executives understand the expectations that are associated with a specific role [60, 95]. Considering this situation, we derived a set of role expectations (based on the CIO responsibilities that are listed in Table 1). Thus, using these role expectations may help alleviate the problem of misunderstandings of expectations. In addition, to measure these expectations, we adopted example performance metrics proposed by Peppard et al. [95] in a way so that these metrics fit with our CIO roles. Table 2 summarizes the expectations and performance metrics that are associated with our six CIO roles.

Table 2 Measuring CIO role effectiveness

CIO role	Major expectations associated with the role	Performance metrics (examples)
Technology provider	• Users possess adequate IT tools to do their job • Electronic linkages are established throughout the firm • IT costs are reduced through existing infrastructure • New IT systems are developed on time and within budget • Users are satisfied with the IT processes	• Cost control • Efficiency of the IT systems • Service availability of the IT systems • On-time project delivery
Strategic supporter	• Investments in IT are aligned with strategic business priorities • Technical solutions to important business problems are designed • Changes in business strategy or processes are immediately addressed by the IT • The IT infrastructure supports future business needs	• IT-business alignment maturity • IT contribution to the business
Business thinker	• Emerging technologies are considered for the business • Business processes and management models are enabled through IT • The TMT understands the capabilities and value of IT • Pilot projects demonstrate the potential of IT • Existing IT performance levels are maintained	• Accomplishing defined service levels • Number of business process improvements • Number of pilot projects
Innovator driver	• Competitive differentiation is achieved through IT innovations • Valuable technical opportunities are delivered for business success • Human, financial, and information resources are allocated for strategic IT initiatives • Employees experiment with new technologies	• Value of developed innovations • Requests for additional services
Integration advisor	• IT assets are leveraged by maintaining existing IT infrastructure • IT innovations are migrated into business processes • The business is empowered with IT capabilities • IT infrastructure meets important technical standards • Valuable information for decision-making is provided	• Return-on-investment from IT spending • Stability of IT infrastructure • Degree of IT standardization
Relationship manager	• Frequent contact with suppliers, customers, buyers, and market analysts • Sourcing strategy meets business objectives and technological needs • Organizational IT requirements are coordinated • Technical standards and policies are defined • Security and privacy is ensured	• IT service availability • Customer and user satisfaction with IT • Technology responsiveness

The role expectations and performance metrics presented in Table 2 can be either used for each role independently or jointly when different roles are used in combination. For example, when a CIO operates as technology provider and relationship manager, then the CIO has to fulfill the expectations of both roles, and also both performance metrics should be applied. As an example for performance metrics, if a CIO acts in the role of a technology provider, then cost control and on-time project delivery are appropriate performance measures; however, if a CIO acts as a relationship manager, then IT service availability or user satisfaction are important measures.

Methodological Observations As a first methodological conclusion, our review provides insight into the use frequency of research methods in CIO research. For all 98 studies that form the database of the present review, we documented the research method, sample size, and country of investigation (see the table in Appendix E). With respect to the use frequency of methods, we found the following results: survey (50 papers), interview (17 papers), case study (7 papers), secondary data analysis (4 papers), mixed methods (5 papers), and miscellaneous (4 papers; this category includes event study, focus groups, and observation). Moreover, we identified 11 conceptual papers. It follows that survey and interview have been by far the most dominant methods in more than three decades of CIO research, while other methods such as case study or secondary data analysis were applied less frequently. Against the background of these results, we make an explicit call for more case studies and research based on secondary data analysis. For example, research can use the annual reports of corporations to gain insight into important business metrics and organizational characteristics (for more information about the use of annual reports as secondary data source see Riedl et al. [112] and Hütter and Riedl [52]).

Another methodological conclusion that can be drawn from our analysis is that mixed methods research is seldom applied in the CIO domain; yet, a few notable examples exist. For example, Peppard et al. [94] applied interview, case study, and focus group to study value-creation for IS investments from an organizational perspective (as opposed to an IS functional perspective). As another example, De Haas and Van Grembergen [23] combined Delphi research and case study to examine IT governance implementations and their impact on business/IT alignment. However, these few mixed methods studies must not hide the fact that a significant research gap exists. This is problematic because a recent paper by Venkatesh et al. [131] outlines the enormous value of mixed methods research in the IS discipline. Specifically, the Venkatesh et al. study indicates seven purposes of mixed methods research (see Table 1 in their paper, p. 26), several of which are also of high relevance in the CIO domain. For example, completeness (i.e. mixed methods are used in order to gain complementary views about the same phenomenon or relationships), compensation (i.e., mixed methods enable compensating for the weaknesses of one approach by using the other), and diversity (i.e., mixed methods are used with the hope of obtaining divergent view of the same phenomenon) are essential purposes for mixed methods studies.

As indicated, we found that survey and interview dominate in CIO research, and considering the potential weaknesses of self-reported data (e.g., social desirability, memory distortion, or informant bias) we argue that future studies should be more frequently conceptualized as mixed methods studies, combining different types of data sets (e.g., self-report, observational, archival). Such a methodological shift is likely to result in novel insights into the antecedents of CIO effectiveness in consideration of different organizational roles.

By analyzing the country in which previous CIO studies collected their data, it becomes evident that CIO research has been predominantly performed in the United States and a few other English-speaking countries (e.g., Australia, Canada, and the United Kingdom). Because both cultural aspects and legal regulations may affect the creation of a CIO position, as well as CIOs and other TMT members' behavior, we make a call for more culturally diverse CIO studies. First, more research is needed in countries which have been mostly neglected in prior studies (e.g., CIO research in the German-speaking area is scarce [52, 112]). Second, investigations with a direct focus on potential differences in antecedents of CIO role effectiveness are urgently needed. One of the few existing studies in this domain [51] found that little variability exists in CIO roles across different cultures (CIOs from New Zealand, Taiwan, and the United States were compared). However, before more definitive conclusions can be drawn, we recommend replications of this finding based on different methods (the Hunter study used interview) and based on different sets of countries.

Moreover, our results indicate a paucity of research that considers the longitudinal nature of CIO effectiveness. Importantly, as revealed by our documentation of methods in Table E.1 (Appendix E), most of the existing literature is based on cross-sectional data collected with interviews and surveys. Furthermore, many case studies in the CIO literature do not constitute true longitudinal studies. Against this background, we make a call for more longitudinal studies (e.g., based on longitudinal case study designs or secondary data analysis), which are better suited to establishing cause-effect relationships.

5.2 Practical Implications

The members of the TMT, particularly the CEO, as well as the supervisory board, are responsible for selecting the CIO role within their organization and for defining suitable performance metrics for the selected role. Due to the ambiguity surrounding the CIO roles, along with the controversial discussion of their responsibilities in academic literature and practitioner magazines, top managers often struggle with the selection of the CIO role and the definition of associated performance metrics [51, 93]. Figure 4 provides a guideline for top managers and supervisory boards.

As a starting point for the CIO role selection process, decision-makers (i.e., top managers or supervisory boards) should consider the scope and responsibilities related to each CIO role (see Table 1) in order to determine which of these roles

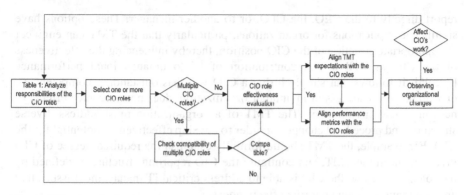

Fig. 4 CIO role selection process

harmonize with their ideas and desires about the IT function within the organization. For example, if the decision-makers want the CIO to use IT as a means to
change existing business processes, a business thinker role should be selected. Due
to the wealth of different responsibilities with which current CIOs have to deal,
some CIOs might be called upon to operate in multiple roles. Consequently,
decision-makers may decide to apply two or more roles to their CIO. However,
as indicated in Fig. 3, not all six roles are compatible and hence decision-makers are
advised to avoid selecting two or more incompatible CIO roles. For example, a
technology provider role is hardly compatible with the innovation driver role. Once
compatible CIO roles have been selected, the role(s) have to be implemented in the
organization, and appropriate expectations that are associated with the selected role(s)
have to be specified. Thereby, it is important that the expectations are aligned with
the performance metrics of the CIO roles (see Table 2). Any misalignment between
role expectations and performance metrics may result in role conflict,
underperformance, and even dismissal of the CIO [38, 62]. Misalignment may
also constrain organizations in their efforts to optimize value derived from their
IT investments [60]. Finally, we recommend that decision-makers continuously
observe organizational and environmental changes which might lead to CIO role
adjustments, and hence the flow model in Fig. 4 starts with a new cycle.

In this context, Leidner and Mackay [73] stress that top managers' expectations
of a new hire are typically framed by the experiences they developed with the
previous incumbent. Hence, the expectations of the new CIO are influenced by
perceptions related to the previous CIO. It is important, therefore, that top managers
do not confuse prior experiences and future orientation too much. Rather, they
should consider a change in the CIO position as a chance to redefine the role of IT
within the organization, and therefore also to redefine the role of the CIO.

In line with this discussion, different CIO roles require differences in the
organizational environment in which the role is implemented. The TMT members
have the authority to directly control or change the CIO's organizational environment in a variety of ways. For example, the TMT can determine the level of the
CIO's formal participation in TMT team meetings, and can require the CIO to

report directly to the CEO, the CFO, or to another manager. These options have significant implications for organizations, particularly that the TMT can engineer the appropriate structure of the CIO position, thereby influencing the effectiveness of the CIO as well as the contribution of IT to organizational performance [73, 95]. It follows that simply hiring a CIO who has outstanding competencies, or who has been successful in another organization, does not guarantee effectiveness in a new environment. The TMT of an organization must address diverse structural and procedural changes in order to develop effectiveness potential for the CIO. For example, the TMT should formally establish the required degree of CIO involvement in the TMT, and configure the CIO reporting structure as defined by the role in order that the CIO is able to address critical IT management issues that are important for achieving role effectiveness.

If the TMT has failed to set up an appropriate working environment, the CIO should lobby the CEO and other executives to align the working environment with the antecedents of CIO role effectiveness as discussed in Sect. 5. Further, the CIO may also conduct educational sessions to leverage the IT understanding of the top managers, and thus trigger changes in the working environment. If no changes are evident, the CIO should accept the existing structure and work to ensure effective communication with the CEO and other executives who perform functions crucial for CIO role effectiveness.

6 Future Research

While our review shows that research has already started to acknowledge the importance of organizational roles for understanding CIO effectiveness, research gaps still exist. As indicated in Fig. 3, all six CIO roles are not compatible with each other. The compatibility of the different CIO roles, however, is currently not a research topic in the IS literature. Thus, empirical research is encouraged to examine our proposal in Fig. 3. Furthermore, Table 2 indicates that each CIO role is associated with specific role expectations and performance metrics. What is still unclear is when compatible CIO roles are applied together, whether additional role expectations and performance metrics gain in significance. For example, if the roles of technology provider and strategic supporter are applied in combination, a new expectation could be that the IT is aligned with the business at a minimum cost. Based on such possible new expectations, new CIO performance measures need to be developed and empirically validated.

Moreover, research is needed to examine in more detail how and why CIOs can translate the opportunities provided by organizational and structural power into performance outcomes. For example, due to the dearth of research on the governance of IT in the context of different CIO roles, we only discussed whether IT governance is necessary for a specific role. Researchers can enhance our approach to gain insights about what type of IT governance structure is appropriate for each role. Weill [136] proposes six mutually exclusive governance archetypes, namely business monarchy, IT monarchy, federal, feudal, IT duopoly, and anarchy. These governance archetypes can serve as a firm foundation for a detailed analysis of the effect of IT governance structure on CIO role effectiveness.

Based on our literature review, we identified four salient CIO role effectiveness antecedents. Despite the fact that we identified these constructs as key determinants of CIO role effectiveness in papers which deal with different CIO roles (see Fig. 2), it is hoped that future empirical research will add further constructs to the model. For example, researchers could add the competitive environment of an organization, including its competitors, vendors, suppliers, and customers, as a fifth antecedent of CIO role effectiveness. Further, the CIO compensation is another antecedent that could be considered in future research as a driver for job effectiveness because a higher salary may motivate CIOs to accomplish specific responsibilities more conscientiously, and this, in turn, may positively influence firm performance [106, 143]. Also, it has been pointed out that IT attention from the board of directors is relevant to CIO effectiveness [50].

Also, the personal competencies that a CIO should possess could be expanded in future research, and CIO experience or CIO functional background may serve as examples [21, 122]. A paper by Leidner and Mackay [73] suggests that CIO experience has a potential impact on CIO role effectiveness, and therefore organizations have to decide carefully whether to select an internal hire or an external hire. An internal candidate knows the structure and processes of the organization, while someone from outside may have a different view on the processes and may better identify opportunities to implement new processes and IT systems.

Altogether, some mentioned constructs for future research have already been discussed in the CIO literature, but their relationship with CIO roles has not yet been empirically established. Future studies could, therefore, investigate a firm's competitive environment, CIO compensation, IT attention of the board of directors, CIO experience, or CIO functional background as antecedents of CIO role effectiveness based on our six roles (see Table 1).

Despite our comprehensive review of the literature, we could not identify any study which explicitly tests the effects of CIO role effectiveness on its immediate antecedents (i.e., the main dependent construct may become an independent construct, which, in turn, affects the originally independent constructs that may be conceptualized as dependent constructs in future research). While speculative in nature, based on our personal experience and informal conversations with CIOs, we assume that CIO role effectiveness is likely to influence some constructs in our model, such as CIO hierarchical position, the management environment, and eventually also the IT infrastructure of the organization in which the CIO operates. If the members of the TMT perceive a CIO's contribution to organizational success, then the TMT may increasingly invite the CIO to TMT meetings or may change the CIO reporting structure and let the CIO report to the CEO, or to another executive manager. When the TMT perceives CIO role effectiveness, then they may also further invest in the IT infrastructure. Thus, research based on various methods is urgently needed to develop an empirical foundation for understanding how CIO role effectiveness influences the other factors in our theoretical model. It is possible that reciprocal effects will be found.

Mintzberg's [88] general management role model proposes that the role classifications are common to all managerial positions, regardless of their functional or hierarchical level. According to this point of view, the CIO role effectiveness model that we have conceptualized in this paper could be used by other research disciplines as a foundation for investigating the effectiveness of positions like the CFO. Over the past decades, the evolving capital markets led to major changes in the roles and responsibilities of the CFO (similar to the CIO), and therefore, a re-conceptualization of the CFO roles and key success factors could be necessary (e.g., [34, 46]). Also, research on CFO role effectiveness could be used to enhance the model of CIO role effectiveness to identify possible mediators or moderators (e.g., trust could be potential mediator or moderator).

Finally, future research could study the relationship between CIO roles and the role of the IT function in organizations. Guillemette and Paré [39], for example, developed and empirically validated five distinct "ideal" IT management profiles in organizations ("Partner", "Systems Provider", "Architecture Builder", "Technological Leader", and "Project Coordinator"). As another example, Kaarst-Brown [60], based on field evidence, developed five clusters of assumptions about IT ("A Necessary Evil", "IT is Support, Not a Partner", "IT rules!", "Business Can do IT Better", and "Equal Partners"). Thus, an important research question with enormous practical relevance is whether CIO roles can be, and should be, distinguished from the roles of IT function in organizations.

7   Concluding Statement

More than three decades of IS research have demonstrated that the CIO is important for organizational success. Further, research has developed various descriptions of the different organizational roles in which a CIO can operate, and has developed models to better understand how CIOs can achieve effectiveness in their roles. Despite the individual value of each single investigation, an integrative view on CIO role effectiveness does not exist. To close this research gap, we reviewed 98 CIO papers in order to develop a set of six CIO organizational roles for the contemporary management, and to develop a model that integrates the key antecedents that are essential for understanding the CIO effectiveness in the developed roles. Based on our model, we explained how and why CIOs achieve effectiveness in their roles, and suggested potential avenues for future research in the CIO domain. It is hoped that our review will result in novel insights, providing a basis for a better understanding of the effectiveness of the CIO whose roles have become significantly diversified since the 1980s.

Acknowledgments We would like to thank Dorothy Leidner and Guillermo Rodríguez Abitia, as well as seven anonymous reviewers for their work in providing guidance on ways to improve earlier versions of this paper.

Appendix A: Related Work on CIO Role Effectiveness

Table A.1 Related work on CIO role effectiveness

Publication	Method/Sample	Applied theory	Abstract/Major findings
Al-Taie et al. [1]	Survey/162 senior IT executives	• Contingency approach to leadership • General management role model	Using the contingency approach to leadership, this paper investigated the influence of an organization's strategic IT vision on both CIO roles and CIO structural power. The survey data shows that the strategic IT vision of an organization influences the CIO roles, and that there is significant positive association between the IT vision and the CIO's structural power in terms of reporting structure and CIO job title
Chen and Wu [18]	Survey/152 matched-paid CIOs and CEOs	• Empowerment theory • Role-based performance theory	Viewed from the perspective of the activity competency model, the authors developed a conceptual framework for investigating the capability of IT management personnel and its impact on the performance of a CIO in eight different roles. The survey data from CIOs and CEOs demonstrate that both IT competencies and managerial competencies have a positive impact on CIO role performance through the IT management capability of the CIO
Chun and Mooney [20]	Interview/17 CIOs		The authors investigated how the CIO's job has changed and evolved over the past decades. Based on interview data, they argue that the

(continued)

Table A.1 (continued)

Publication	Method/Sample	Applied theory	Abstract/Major findings
			CIO's role has evolved over the past decades to reflect both the firm's IT infrastructure and the firm's IT strategy. The degree to which a firm has standardized its IT infrastructure, and the degree to which IT enables core products, services, or processes of the firm, influence the nature of the CIO role
Grover et al. [38]	Survey/71 CIOs and 40 IT middle manager	• General management role model	This paper examined six managerial roles of the CIO based on Mintzberg's general managerial role model. The survey data indicate that CIOs differ from manufacturing and sales executives in the relative importance they place on managerial roles. This difference does not exist between CIOs and finance executives or between CIOs and IT managers. Further, the results indicate that both the maturity of the organization's IT management and the degree of centralization of the IT resource determine the importance of the different CIO roles
Leidner and Mackay [73]	Interview/36 CIOs		During the first year on the job, incoming CIOs use diverse approaches to establish their credibility and to provide value to their firms. The authors categorized the transition approaches of CIOs as either incremental or radical. Incremental means that during the first year, CIOs initiated change in only one major area at a time (IT human resources, IT processes, IT infrastructure, or IT relationship with the business). Radical means that within the first year, CIOs simultaneously initiated change in at least three of the four major areas. Based on interview data, the authors found that CIOs choice of transition approach is closely associated with the IT leader visibility of their predecessor

(continued)

Table A.1 (continued)

Publication	Method/Sample	Applied theory	Abstract/Major findings
Li et al. [75]	Survey/129 matched-pair CIOs and business executives	• General management role model • Upper echelons theory	The authors draw upon the upper echelon theory to investigate the relationship between CIO role effectiveness and organizational innovative use of IT. The survey data show that the intensity of relationship between strategic CIO role effectiveness and organizational innovative use of IT is much stronger in organizations that articulate a transform IT vision. However, operational CIO role effectiveness was not found to have significant impact on organizational innovative use of IT across all IT visions (this relationship is completely mediated by strategic CIO role effectiveness)
Peppard et al. [95]	Interview/26 CIOs, 12 CxOs, 2 recruiters, and 2 industry analysts and commentators		To better understand the CIO roles, together with the causes and consequences of ambiguity surrounding these roles, the authors conducted interviews with various managers. Their findings indicate that present CIOs operate in five different roles. The appropriate role for a particular organization at a point in time is determined by the criticality of IT for its competitive differentiation and the maturity of its IT leadership capabilities. Both factors are strongly influenced by the digital literacy of the TMT
Preston et al. [103]	Survey/174 matched-pair CIOs and top managers		Organizations invest in IT initiatives to improve their level of performance, but the results from the payoff of IT investments are mixed. This paper presents evidence that the variation in benefits derived from IT depends on the firm's CIO leadership profile. This profile is determined by whether the CIO's level of strategic decision-making authority is high or low, and whether the CIO's strategic leadership capability is high or low. Based on survey data, the authors show that the level of IT contribution to a firm's

(continued)

Table A.1 (continued)

Publication	Method/Sample	Applied theory	Abstract/Major findings
			performance varies according to the CIO leadership profile
Ross and Feeny [115]	Conceptual/n. a.	• Organizational learning	This paper historically analyzed the forces that have shaped the CIO roles in organizations over the past decades in order to explain the current responsibilities of the CIO and to discuss how the CIO role might evolve
Smaltz et al. [120]	Survey/100 matched-pair CIOs and top managers	• General management role model • Role-based performance • Upper echelons theory	Despite a wealth of research about what roles CIOs should play in contemporary firms, there has been limited empirical research on the antecedents of CIO effectiveness in those roles. Based on survey data from CIOs and top managers, the authors argue that the CIO capabilities, in the form of business and strategic IT knowledge, political savvy, and interpersonal communication, makes CIOs effective. The results further indicate that high levels of CIO/TMT engagements do not directly impact CIO role effectiveness, but are mediated by the effects of CIO capabilities
Weill and Woerner [139]	Mixed methods/n. a.		CIO activities are expanding from providing IT services to including external customer responsibilities, working with non-IT managers, and managing enterprise processes. Therefore, the authors identified emerging key activities for four types of CIOs, and then analyzed how CIOs spend their time across these activities. Further, they analyzed the most important governance mechanism for those four CIO types

Note: n. a. = not applicable

Appendix B: Analyzed Papers in the IS Literature

Table B.1 Papers relevant for CIO role effectiveness

Journals and conference proceedings	Relevant to CIO role effectiveness
California Management Review	3
Decision Sciences	1
IEEE Transactions on Engineering Management	6
Information and Management	9
Information Systems Journal	1
Information Systems Research	3
Information Systems Management	4
International Journal of Information Management	2
Journal of Business Research	1
Journal of Information Technology	2
Journal of Management Information Systems	8
Journal of Strategic Information Systems	2
MIS Quarterly	23
MIS Quarterly Executive	10
Omega	2
Proceedings of the Americas Conference on Information Systems	2
Proceedings of the Australasian Conference on Information Systems	2
Proceedings of the International Conference on Information Systems	3
Proceedings of the Pacific Asia Conference on Information Systems	2
Sloan Management Review	6
Other	6
Total	**98**

© The Author(s) 2017

A. Hütter, R. Riedl, *Chief Information Officer Role Effectiveness*, SpringerBriefs in Information Systems, DOI 10.1007/978-3-319-54753-4

Appendix C: Conceptualization of the CIO Roles

Table C.1 Categorization of the CIO roles[a]

Publication	CIO role in the literature	Description of the CIO role	Mapped to category
Grover et al. [38]	Entrepreneur	"…identifies business needs and develops solutions that change business situations." (p. 112)	Business thinker
	Leader	"…supervising, hiring, training, and motivating a cadre of specialized personnel." (p. 110)	Innovation driver
	Liaison	"…communicate with the external environment including exchanging information with IS suppliers, customers, buyers, market analysts, and the media." (p. 112)	Relationship manager
	Monitor	"…scan the external environment to keep up with technical changes and competition." (p. 112)	Integration advisor
	Resource allocator	"…decide how to allocate human, financial, and information resources." (p. 112)	Technology provider
	Spokesman	"…extend organizational contacts outside the department to other areas of the organization." (p. 111)	Strategic supporter
Ross and Feeny [115]	Business visionary	"…one of the main drivers of strategy by recognizing the emerging capabilities and applications of information technology, and arguing their significance to the business." (p. 399)	Business thinker
	Functional head	"…developing new systems to time and budget; achieving the ROI expected when the investment was approved; and operating the portfolio of developed systems to the agreed service levels and satisfaction of the user community." (p. 398)	Technology provider
	Strategic partner	"…designing and developing a complex IT organization that can address immediate business needs while building an infrastructure that supports ongoing needs as well." (p. 399)	Strategic supporter

(continued)

© The Author(s) 2017
A. Hütter, R. Riedl, *Chief Information Officer Role Effectiveness*, SpringerBriefs
in Information Systems, DOI 10.1007/978-3-319-54753-4

Table C.1 (continued)

Publication	CIO role in the literature	Description of the CIO role	Mapped to category
Smaltz et al. [120]	Information steward	"...organizational steward for high quality data and operationally reliable systems." (p. 216)	Integration advisor
	Integrator	"...providing leadership in enterprise-wide integration of processes, information, and decision-support as digital options for the business." (p. 216)	Integration advisor
	IT educator	"...IT missionary, who provides insights and understanding about key information technol-ogies is critical." (p. 216)	Business thinker
	Relationship architect	"...build relationships both across the enter-prise as well as outside the enterprise with key IT services providers..." (p. 216)	Relationship manager
	Strategist	"...be effective business partners and help their organizations leverage valuable opportu-nities for IT-based innovation and business process redesign." (p. 216)	Innovation driver
	Utilities provider	"...building and sustaining a solid, depend-able, and responsive IT infrastructure ser-vices." (p. 216)	Technology provider
Leidner and Mackay [73]	Big-bang CIO	"...implementation of one or more large organization-wide applications intended to fundamentally improve organizational perfor-mance." (p. 21)	Business thinker
	Keep-it-run-ning CIO	"...reducing the cost of IT, while paying less attention to championing major new systems." (p. 21)	Technology provider
	Value-adding CIO	"...overseeing the development of new, or enhancements to existing, systems that are intended to address a business unit need." (p.21)	Strategic supporter
Preston et al. [103]	IT advisor	"...has limited decision-making authority but is a highly capable leader with vast strategic knowledge who may be well suited to serve as a strategic advisor to the top management team on IT issues." (p. 64)	Integration advisor
	IT laggard	"...are provided with a relatively high level of decision-making authority, but they do not have the requisite leadership skills to capitalize on the strategic authority provided to them." (p. 64)	Strategic supporter
	IT mechanic	"...have a low level of both strategic effec-tiveness and strategic decision-making authority." (p. 62)	Technology provider
	IT orchestrator	"...effective strategic leader who is granted a great deal of freedom in making strategic decisions." (p. 61)	Innovation driver

(continued)

Table C.1 (continued)

Publication	CIO role in the literature	Description of the CIO role	Mapped to category
Chun and Mooney [20]	Innovator and creator	"...innovation and new opportunities, implementing new IS across the corporation." (p. 330)	Innovation driver
	Landscape cultivator	"...technical improvement and rationalization of the firm's data by maintaining and integrating existing applications and processes." (p. 330)	Integration advisor
	Opportunity seeker	"...improve business processes within and outside the firm." (p.330)	Business thinker
	Triage nurse and firefighter	"...fix urgent IS-related problems (e.g., technical bugs, failed systems and disrupted processing)." (p. 330)	Technology provider
Chen and Wu [18]	Business visionary	"...lead the executive team in developing a business vision that captures the opportunities presented by IT." (p. 148)	Business thinker
	Business system thinker	"...think through new business models and introduce new management processes that leverage the emerging/enabling IT..." (p. 148)	Business thinker
	Entrepreneur	"...identify business needs and develops solutions that change business situations and ensure that rapidly evolving technical opportunities are...strategically exploited in the organization." (p. 148)	Business thinker
	Informed buyer	"...deploy external resources in a manner that maximized the effectiveness of internal resources and lowered organizational costs." (p. 148)	Relationship manager
	Infrastructure builder	"...create the coherent blueprint for a technical platform/infrastructure which responds to present and future business needs." (p. 148)	Integration advisor
	Organizational designer	"...devise and continuously adapt an IT organization that responded to the business-side (business model/process) realities." (p. 148)	Strategic supporter
	Relationship builder	"...facilitate the wider dialogue, establishing understanding, trust, and cooperation among business users and IT specialists." (p. 148)	Relationship manager
	Value configurer	"...define an organization's strategic future, who has an unrivalled understanding of the ideas that are being deployed throughout the organization and even outside its boundaries." (p. 148)	Innovation driver
Peppard et al. [95]	Agility IT director/CIO	"...supply of technology and systems to support an organization in which demand is being defined as an everyday occurrence by the business." (p. 37)	Relationship manager

(continued)

Table C.1 (continued)

Publication	CIO role in the literature	Description of the CIO role	Mapped to category
	Evangelist CIO	"...raising the profile of information within the organization, 'selling' the idea that information can potentially be leveraged to generate significant business value." (p. 35)	Business thinker
	Facilitator CIO	"...ensuring that information skills and capabilities pervade every part of the organization." (p. 37)	Integration advisor
	Innovator CIO	"...identifies and develops opportunities to deploy new IT-enabled processes and products/services that give the organization a clear source of competitive differentiation..." (p. 35)	Innovation driver
	Utility IT director	"...provide IT infrastructure, systems, data, and telecommunications capability." (p. 35)	Technology provider
Li et al. [75]	Information strategist	"...developing information strategy that aligns with the business strategy." (p. 6)	Integration advisor
	Integrator	"...integrating the enterprise systems across the various business units in all organizations with multiple lines of business since many organizations operate in a highly disassociated manner." (p. 6)	Integration advisor
	IS contract oversight	"...oversight of IS contractual arrangements since more organizations outsource portions of there is services." (p. 6)	Relationship manager
	IS strategist	"...partner with TMT to fully leverage the potential value of IT investments." (p. 6)	Innovation driver
	IT manager	"...operating IT function plan effectively and enabling the development and leveraging of IS human capital." (p. 6)	Technology provider
Weill and Woerner [139]	Embedded CIO	"...being part of the senior leadership team participating daily in strategic conversations and overseeing enterprise-wide business operations." (p. 68)	Innovation driver
	Enterprise processes CIO	"...overseeing and operating key enterprise business processes as well as IT." (p. 69)	Integration advisor
	IT services CIO	"...provide all the IT services the firm needs to operate in a digital economy." (p. 68)	Technology provider
	External customer CIO	"...strengthen the company's relationships with its customers and to help sell and deliver products and services." (p. 70)	Relationship manager

[a]Note that the study from Al-Taie et al. [1] is not included in this list because the authors literally cite the CIO roles from Smaltz et al. [120]

Appendix D: Conceptualization of the CIO Role Effectiveness Model

Table D.1 Constructs important for CIO role effectiveness

Publication	Construct from the literature	Definition of the construct	Mapped to construct
Al-Taie et al. [1]	CIO structural power	"…CIO's level of legitimate power in their formal position within the hierarchy of the organization." (p. 69)	CIO reporting structure
	Organizational vision of IT	"…shared, aspired state of the role that IT should play in the firm." (p. 61)	IT strategy
Chen and Wu [18]	CIO role performance	"…role performance of CIOs in the context of specific roles, behaviors, and responsibilities that are regarded as salient in today's business environment." (p. 149)	CIO role effectiveness
	IT competence	"…levels of skills/knowledge that enable him or her to configure, implement, apply, and evaluate IT, with the purpose of establishing enterprise-wide IT infrastructure, initiate various sorts of business applications, and integrate IT functions with critical business processes." (p. 149)	Technical competence
	Management competence	"…level of skills/knowledge that enabled them to understand the domain-specific knowledge of business, speak the language of business, and interact with their business partners in other divisions." (p. 149)	Business competence
Chun and Mooney [20]	IS strategy	"…represents a continuum of firms that have implemented a stable and risk averse IS strategy through firms that have followed a forward-thinking and risk-taking approach." (p. 330)	IT strategy

© The Author(s) 2017
A. Hütter, R. Riedl, *Chief Information Officer Role Effectiveness*, SpringerBriefs in Information Systems, DOI 10.1007/978-3-319-54753-4

Table D.1 (continued)

Publication	Construct from the literature	Definition of the construct	Mapped to construct
	IS Infrastructure	"...represents a continuum of how firms implemented their IS infrastructures, ranging from those that have many non-standard applications, processes, and functions to those with systemic infrastructures integrated across business processes and organizational units." (p. 330)	IT infrastructure
Grover et al. [38]	IS maturity	"...membership on the TMT...provides the CIO with regular opportunities for engagement with other top managers and is perceived as being effective in addressing the firm's salient IT management and use challenges." (p. 212)	TMT understanding of IT
	IS maturity	"...formalization level of IS control mechanisms, level of user awareness and involvement, availability of strategic IS planning, and the degree to which the setting of IS objectives is rational and compatible with organizational objectives." (p. 114 f.)	IT governance structure
	IS centralization	n. a.	IT strategy
Li et al. [75]	CIO strategic role effectiveness	"...CIO strategic role effectiveness is defined as the top business executives' assessments of the extent to which the CIO leads the entire firm in exploring IT-enabled innovations and new strategic opportunities." (p. 3)	CIO role effectiveness
	CIO operational role effectiveness	"...define CIO operational role effectiveness as the top business executives' assessments of the extent to which the CIO leads the IT function to exploit existing IT resources to meet ongoing known business needs." (p. 3)	CIO role effectiveness
Peppard et al. [95]	Senior management digital literacy	n. a.	TMT understanding of IT
	IT governance	n. a.	IT governance structure
Preston et al., [103]	Strategic IT knowledge	n. a.	IT management competence
	Strategic business knowledge	n. a.	Business competence
	Communication ability	n. a.	Communication competence
	Political savvy	n. a.	Political competence

(continued)

Table D.1 (continued)

Publication	Construct from the literature	Definition of the construct	Mapped to construct
	CIO is a member of the top management team	n. a.	CIO membership in the TMT
	CIO reporting level	n. a.	CIO reporting structure
	Strategic IT vision	n. a.	IT strategy
	Dedication of resources to IT	n. a.	IT strategy
Smaltz et al. [120]	CIO role effectiveness	"CIO Role Effectiveness is the TMT members' assessment of the CIO in the context of specific roles, behaviors, and responsibilities that are regarded as salient in firms." (p. 210)	CIO role effectiveness
	Interpersonal communication skill	"CIO's ability to communicate clearly, persuasively, and in business terms." (p. 211)	Communication competence
	Extent of trusting relationships	"...developing a trusting relationship with the other members of the TMT seems an important dimension of CIO engagements with the TMT." (p. 213)	Political competence
	TMT membership	"...membership on the TMT...provides the CIO with regular opportunities for engagement with other top managers and is perceived as being effective in addressing the firm's salient IT management and use challenges." (p. 212)	CIO membership in the TMT
	Strategic IT knowledge	"Strategic IT knowledge is defined as awareness and understanding about current and emerging information technologies, their relevance for the firm, and insights related to investment timing and acquisition of information technologies." (p. 211)	IT management competence
	Strategic business knowledge	"CIO's strategic business knowledge is defined as the person's understanding and appreciation of their firm's competitive forces and business strategies." (p. 211)	Business competence
	Political savvy	"Political savvy an executive's ability to negotiate, influence, and persuade." (p. 211)	Political competence
Weill and Woerner [139]	IT governance	n. a.	IT governance structure

Note: n. a. = not applicable

Table D.2 Relationships important for CIO role effectiveness

Publication	Nature of the construct in the literature	Relationship mapped to our model
Al-Taie et al. [1]	Organizational vision of IT → CIO roles	IT strategy → CIO role effectiveness
	Organizational vision of IT → CIO structural power	Management environment (IT strategy) → CIO hierarchical position (CIO reporting structure)
Chen and Wu [18]	IT competence → IT management activity effectiveness → CIO role performance	Technical competence → CIO role effectiveness
	Management competence → IT management activity effectiveness → CIO role performance	Business competence → CIO role effectiveness
Chun and Mooney [20]	IS strategy → CIO role evolution	IT strategy → CIO role effectiveness
	IS Infrastructure → CIO role evolution	IT infrastructure → CIO role effectiveness
	IS strategy → IS Infrastructure	Management environment (IT strategy) → IT infrastructure
Grover et al. [38]	IS centralization → Nature of the CIO role	IT strategy → CIO role effectiveness
	IS maturity → Nature of the CIO role	IT governance structure → CIO role effectiveness
Peppard et al. [95]	Senior management digital literacy → CIO role success	TMT understanding of IT → CIO role effectiveness
	IT governance → CIO role success	IT governance structure → CIO role effectiveness
Preston et al. [103]	Strategic IT knowledge → CIO leadership profile	IT management competence → CIO role effectiveness
	Strategic business knowledge → CIO leadership profile	Business competence → CIO role effectiveness
	Communication ability → CIO leadership profile	Communication competence → CIO role effectiveness
	Political savvy → CIO leadership profile	Political competence → CIO role effectiveness
	CIO is a member of the top management team → CIO leadership profile	CIO membership in the TMT → CIO role effectiveness
	CIO reporting level → CIO leadership profile	CIO reporting structure → CIO role effectiveness
	Strategic IT vision → CIO leadership profile	IT strategy → CIO role effectiveness
	Dedication of resources to IT → CIO leadership profile	IT strategy → CIO role effectiveness
Smaltz et al. [120]	Strategic business knowledge → CIO capability → CIO role effectiveness	Business competence → CIO role effectiveness
	Strategic IT knowledge → CIO capability → CIO role effectiveness	IT management competence → CIO role effectiveness

(continued)

Table D.2 (continued)

Publication	Nature of the construct in the literature	Relationship mapped to our model
	Interpersonal communication skill → CIO capability → CIO role effectiveness	Communication competence → CIO role effectiveness
	Political savvy → CIO capability → CIO role effectiveness	Political competence → CIO role effectiveness
	Extent of trusting relationships → CIO capability → CIO role effectiveness	Political competence → CIO role effectiveness
	TMT membership → TMT/CIO engagements → CIO capability → CIO role effectiveness	CIO hierarchical position (CIO membership in the TMT) → CIO personal competence → CIO role effectiveness
Weill and Woerner [139]	IT governance mechanisms → CIO role performance	IT governance structure → CIO role effectiveness

Appendix E: Methodological Conclusion Resulting from Our Review

Table E.1 Research method of papers included in review (N = 98 papers)

Publication	Method	Sample size	Country of investigation
Al-Taie et al. [1]	Survey	162	Australia
Applegate and Elam [2]	Survey	64	United States
Armstrong and Sambamurthy [3]	Survey	153	United States
Banker et al. [5]	Secondary data	258	United States
Bassellier et al. [6]	Survey	404	United States
Bassellier et al. [7]	Survey	111	Canada
Boynton et al. [9]	Survey	132	United States
Broadbent and Weill [11]	Mixed methods	n. a.	n. a.
Broadbent et al. [12]	Case study	26	Asia, Australia, Europe, North America
Broadbent et al. [13]	Case study	4	n. a.
Chan et al. [15]	Survey	170	Canada, United States
Chan et al. [16]	Survey	226	n. a.
Chatterjee et al. [17]	Event study	96	United States
Chen and Wu [18]	Survey	152	China, Taiwan
Chen et al. [19]	Survey	174	United States
Chun and Mooney [20]	Interview	17	United States
Cohen and Dennis [21]	Survey	111	South Africa
Cybulski and Lukaitis [22]	Focus groups	16	Australia
De Haes and Van Grembergen [23]	Mixed methods	n. a.	Belgium
Doll [25]	Interview	33	United States
Earl and Feeny [28]	Interview	60	United States
Earl and Feeny [29]	Conceptual	n. a.	n. a.
Enns et al. [31]	Survey	69	Canada, United States
Enns et al. [32]	Survey	69	Canada, United States
Faraj and Sambamurthy [33]	Survey	333	United States

© The Author(s) 2017
A. Hütter, R. Riedl, *Chief Information Officer Role Effectiveness*, SpringerBriefs
in Information Systems, DOI 10.1007/978-3-319-54753-4

Table E.1 (continued)

Publication	Method	Sample size	Country of investigation
Feeny and Willcocks [35]	Conceptual	n. a.	n. a.
Feeny et al. [36]	Interview	14	United Kingdom
Gottschalk [37]	Survey	471	Norway
Grover et al. [38]	Survey	111	United States
Gupta [40]	Conceptual	n. a.	n. a.
Hooper and Bunker [47]	Interview	17	New Zealand
Huang and Quaddus [49]	Survey	119	Taiwan
Hunter [51]	Interview	18	New Zealand, Taiwan, United States
Ives and Olson [53]	Observation	6	United States
Jarvenpaa and Ives [54]	Survey	55	United States
Johnson and Lederer [55]	Survey	202	United States
Johnson and Lederer [56]	Survey	202	United States
Johnson and Lederer [57]	Survey	202	United States
Johnson and Lederer [58]	Survey	202	United States
Jones et al. [59]	Survey	39	United States
Kaarst-Brown [60]	Case study	2	United States
Karimi et al. [62]	Survey	213	United States
Kearns [63]	Survey	161	United States
Kearns and Lederer [64]	Survey	161	United States
Kearns and Sabherwal [65]	Survey	274	United States
Kettinger et al. [67]	Case study	4	Europe
Lane and Koronios [69]	Survey	46	Australia
Lederer and Mendelow [70]	Interview	20	United States
Lederer and Mendelow [71]	Interview	20	United States
Lee et al. [72]	Survey	98	United States
Leidner and Mackay [73]	Interview	36	United States
Leidner et al. [74]	Interview	20	United States
Li et al. [75]	Survey	126	China
Li and Ye [76]	Secondary data	216	United States
Li and Tan [77]	Survey	81	n. a.
Li et al. [78]	Survey	89	Singapore
Luftman and Brier [79]	Mixed methods	n. a.	United States
Luftman and Kempaiah [80]	Survey	197	Europe, India, Latin America, United States
Maes and De Vries [81]	Conceptual	n. a.	n. a.
Martin [82]	Survey	15	n. a.
Mata et al. [85]	Conceptual	n. a.	n. a.
Nelson and Cooprider [90]	Survey	86	United States
Peppard [93]	Interview	42	Europe
Peppard et al. [94]	Mixed methods	n. a.	n. a.
Peppard et al. [95]	Interview	42	Europe

(continued)

Table E.1 (continued)

Publication	Method	Sample size	Country of investigation
Pervan [96]	Survey	452	Australia
Piccoli and Ives [97]	Conceptual	n. a.	n. a.
Preston and Karahanna [100]	Survey	382	United States
Preston and Karahanna [101]	Survey	243	United States
Preston et al. [102]	Survey	207	France, United States
Preston et al. [103]	Survey	174	United States
Raghunathan and Raghunathan [104]	Survey	192	United States
Ragu-Nathan et al. [105]	Survey	231	United States
Ranganathan and Jha [107]	Secondary data	205	United States
Rathnam et al. [108]	Interview	50	United States
Rattanasampan and Chaidaroon [109]	Conceptual	n. a.	n. a.
Reich and Benbasat [110]	Case study	10	Canada
Reich and Benbasat [111]	Case study	10	Canada
Rockart et al. [113]	Conceptual	n. a.	n. a.
Rockart et al. [114]	Interview	16	Europe, Japan, United States
Ross and Feeny [115]	Conceptual	n. a.	n. a.
Ross et al. [116]	Conceptual	n. a.	n. a.
Sambamurthy et al. [117]	Conceptual	n. a.	n. a.
Sharma and Rai [119]	Survey	350	United States
Smaltz et al. [120]	Survey	100	United States
Sobol and Klein [122]	Survey	92	United States
Spitze and Lee [123]	Interview	14	United States
Stephens et al. [124]	Observation	5	United States
Štemberger et al [125]	Survey	152	Slovenia
Tallon [127]	Survey	241	United States
Tan and Gallupe [128]	Interview	80	New Zealand
Watson [132]	Survey	43	Australia
Watson et al. [133]	Secondary data	n. a.	n. a
Watts and Henderson [134]	Interview	36	United States
Weill [136]	Survey	256	n. a.
Weill and Woerner [139]	Mixed methods	n. a.	n. a.
Willson and Pollard [141]	Case study	1	Australia
Wu et al. [142]	Survey	264	Taiwan

Note: n. a. = not applicable

References

1. Al-Taie, M., Lane, M., Cater-Steel, A.: The relationship between organisational strategic IT vision and CIO roles: one size does not fit all. Australas. J. Inf. Syst. **18**(2), 59–89 (2014)
2. Applegate, L.M., Elam, J.J.: New information systems leaders: a changing role in a changing world. MIS Q. **16**(4), 469–490 (1992)
3. Armstrong, C.P., Sambamurthy, V.: Information technology assimilation in firms: the influence of senior leadership and IT infrastructures. Inf. Syst. Res. **10**(4), 304–327 (1999)
4. Astley, W.G., Sachdeva, P.S.: Structural sources of intraorganizational power: a theoretical synthesis. Acad. Manage. Rev. **9**(1), 104–113 (1984)
5. Banker, R.D., Hu, N., Pavlou, P.A., Luftman, J.: CIO reporting structure, strategic positioning, and firm performance. MIS Q. **35**(2), 487–504 (2011)
6. Bassellier, G., Benbasat, I., Reich, B.H.: The influence of business managers' IT competence on championing IT. Inf. Syst. Res. **14**(4), 317–336 (2003)
7. Bassellier, G., Gagnon, E., Pinsonneault, A.: CIO and CEO heterogeneity, IT support, and IT competitiveness in stable and unstable environments: an empirical study. In: Proceedings of the 14th Americas Conference on Information Systems, paper 194 (2008)
8. Bock, G., Carpenter, K., Davis, J.E.: Management's newest star: meet the chief information officer. Bus. Week. **2968**, 160–172 (1986)
9. Boynton, A.C., Zmud, R.W., Jacobs, G.C.: The influence of IT management practice on IT use in large organizations. MIS Q. **18**(3), 299–318 (1994)
10. Broadbent, M., Kitzis, E.: The New CIO Leader: Setting the Agenda and Delivering Results. Harvard Business School Press, Boston (2005)
11. Broadbent, M., Weill, P.: Management by maxim: how business and IT managers can create IT infrastructures. Sloan Manage. Rev. **38**(3), 77–92 (1997)
12. Broadbent, M., Weill, P., Neo, B.S.: Strategic context and patterns of IT infrastructure capability. J. Strateg. Inf. Syst. **8**(2), 157–187 (1999)
13. Broadbent, M., Weill, P., St. Clair, D.: The implications of information technology infrastructure for business process redesign. MIS Q. **23**(2), 159–182 (1999)
14. Burke, P.J.: Identity process and social stress. Am. Sociol. Rev. **56**(6), 836–849 (1991)
15. Chan, Y.E., Huff, S.L., Barclay, D.W., Copeland, D.G.: Business strategic orientation, information systems strategic orientation, and strategic alignment. Inf. Syst. Res. **8**(2), 125–150 (1997)
16. Chan, Y.E., Sabherwal, R., Thatcher, J.B.: Antecedents and outcomes of strategic IS alignment: an empirical investigation. IEEE Trans. Eng. Manage. **53**(1), 27–47 (2006)

© The Author(s) 2017

A. Hütter, R. Riedl, *Chief Information Officer Role Effectiveness*, SpringerBriefs in Information Systems, DOI 10.1007/978-3-319-54753-4

17. Chatterjee, D., Richardson, V.J., Zmud, R.W.: Examining the shareholder wealth effects of announcements of newly created CIO positions. MIS Q. **25**(1), 43–70 (2001)

18. Chen, Y.-C., Wu, J.-H.: IT management capability and its impact on the performance of a CIO. Inf. Manage. **48**(4/5), 145–156 (2011)

19. Chen, D.Q., Preston, D.S., Xia, W.: Antecedents and effects of CIO supply-side and demand-side leadership: a staged maturity model. J. Manage. Inf. Syst. **27**(1), 231–271 (2010)

20. Chun, M., Mooney, J.: CIO roles and responsibilities: twenty-five years of evolution and change. Inf. Manage. **46**(6), 323–334 (2009)

21. Cohen, J.F., Dennis, C.M.: Chief information officers: an empirical study of competence, organisational positioning and implications for performance. S. Afr. J. Econ. Manage. Sci. **13** (2), 203–221 (2010)

22. Cybulski, J., Lukaitis, St.: The impact of communications and understanding on the success of business/IT alignment. In: Proceedings of the 16th Australasian Conference on Information Systems, paper 98 (2005)

23. De Haes, S., Van Grembergen, W.: An exploratory study into IT governance implementations and its impact on business/IT alignment. Inf. Syst. Manage. **26**(2), 123–137 (2009)

24. Dibbern, J., Goles, T., Hirschheim, R., Jayatilaka, B.: Information systems outsourcing: a survey and analysis of the literature. ACM SIGMIS Database. **35**(4), 6–102 (2004)

25. Doll, W.J.: Avenues for top management involvement in successful MIS development. MIS Q. **9**(1), 17–35 (1985)

26. Duncan, N.B.: Capturing flexibility of information technology infrastructure: a study of resource characteristics and their measure. J. Manage. Inf. Syst. **12**(2), 37–57 (1995)

27. Earl, M.J.: The chief information officer: past, present and future. In: Earl, M.J. (ed.) Information Management: The Organizational Dimension. Oxford University Press, Oxford (1996)

28. Earl, M.J., Feeny, D.F.: Is your CIO adding value? Sloan Manage. Rev. **35**(3), 11–20 (1994)

29. Earl, M.J., Feeny, D.F.: How to be a CEO for the information age. Sloan Manage. Rev. **41**(2), 11–23 (2000)

30. Eisenhardt, K.M., Zbaracki, M.J.: Strategic decision making. Strateg. Manage. J. **13**(2), 17–37 (1992)

31. Enns, H.G., Huff, S.L., Higgins, C.A.: CIO lateral influence behaviors: gaining peers' commitment to strategic information systems. MIS Q. **27**(1), 155–176 (2003)

32. Enns, H.G., Huff, S.L., Golden, B.R.: CIO influence behaviors: the impact of technical background. Inf. Manage. **40**(5), 467–485 (2003)

33. Faraj, S., Sambamurthy, V.: Leadership of information systems development projects. IEEE Trans. Eng. Manage. **53**(2), 238–249 (2006)

34. Favaro, P.: Beyond bean counting: the CFO's expanding role. Strateg. Leadersh. **29**(5), 4–8 (2001)

35. Feeny, D.F., Willcocks, L.P.: Core IS capabilities for exploiting information technology. Sloan Manage. Rev. **39**(3), 9–21 (1998)

36. Feeny, D.F., Edwards, B.R., Simpson, M.K.: Understanding the CEO/CIO relationship. MIS Q. **16**(4), 435–448 (1992)

37. Gottschalk, P.: Strategic management of IS/IT functions: the role of the CIO in Norwegian organisations. Int. J. Inf. Manage. **19**(5), 389–399 (1999)

38. Grover, V., Seung-Ryul, J., Kettinger, W.J., Lee, C.C.: The chief information officer: a study of managerial roles. J. Manage. Inf. Syst. **10**(2), 107–130 (1993)

39. Guillemette, M.G., Paré, G.: Toward a new theory of the contribution of the IT function in organizations. MIS Q. **36**(2), 529–551 (2012)

40. Gupta, Y.P.: The chief executive officer and the chief information officer: the strategic partnership. J. Inf. Technol. **6**(3/4), 128–139 (1991)

41. Hambrick, D.C., Mason, P.A.: Upper echelons: the organization as a reflection of its top managers. Acad. Manage. Rev. **9**(2), 193–206 (1984)

42. Hambrick, D.C.: Upper echelons theory: an update. Acad. Manage. Rev. **32**(2), 334–343 (2007)
43. Hanseth, O., Monteiro, E., Hatling, M.: Developing information infrastructure: the tension between standardization and flexibility. Sci. Technol. Hum. Values. **21**(4), 407–426 (1996)
44. Hirschheim, R., Porra, J., Parks, M.S.: The evolution of the corporate IT function and the role of the CIO at Texaco: how do perceptions of IT's performance get formed? DATA BASE Adv. Inf. Syst. **34**(4), 8–27 (2003)
45. Hollmann, T.: The meanings of competency. J. Eur. Ind. Train. **23**(6), 275–286 (1999)
46. Hommel, U., Fabich, M., Schellenberg, E., Firnkorn, L.: The Strategic CFO: Creating Value in a Dynamic Market Environment. Springer, Heidelberg (2012)
47. Hooper, V., Bunker, B.: The role and requisite competencies of the public sector CIO: a two-sided perspective. Electron. J. Inf. Syst. Eval. **16**(3), 188–199 (2013)
48. Horlacher, A., Hess, T.: What does a chief digital officer do? Managerial tasks and roles of a new C-level position in the context of digital transformation. In: Proceedings of the 49th Hawaii International Conference on System Sciences, Hawaii, 5126–5135 (2016)
49. Huang, K., Quaddus, M.: An analysis of IT expectations across different strategic context of innovation: the CEO versus the CIO. In: Proceedings of the Pacific Asia Conference on Information Systems, paper 190 (2008)
50. Huff, S.L., Maher, M., Munro, M.C.: Information technology and the board of directors: is there an IT attention deficit? MIS Q. Exec. **5**(2), 55–68 (2006)
51. Hunter, G.: The chief information officer: a review of the role. J. Inf. Inf. Technol. Organ. **5**(1), 125–143 (2010)
52. Hütter, A., Riedl, R.: Der Chief Information Officer (CIO) in Deutschland und den USA: Verbreitung und Unterschiede. Inf. Manage. Consult. **26**(3), 61–66 (2011)
53. Ives, B., Olson, M.H.: Manager or technician? The nature of the information systems manager's job. MIS Q. **5**(4), 49–63 (1981)
54. Jarvenpaa, S.L., Ives, B.: Executive involvement and participation in the management of information technology. MIS Q. **15**(2), 205–227 (1991)
55. Johnson, A.M., Lederer, A.L.: The effect of communication frequency and channel richness on the convergence between chief executive and chief information officers. J. Manage. Inf. Syst. **22**(2), 227–252 (2005)
56. Johnson, A.M., Lederer, A.L.: The impact of communication between CEOs and CIOs on their shared views of the current and future role of IT. Inf. Syst. Manage. **24**(1), 85–90 (2007)
57. Johnson, A.M., Lederer, A.L.: CEO/CIO mutual understanding, strategic alignment, and the contribution of IS to the organization. Inf. Manage. **47**(3), 138–149 (2010)
58. Johnson, A.M., Lederer, A.L.: IS strategy and IS contribution: CEO and CIO perspectives. Inf. Syst. Manage. **30**(4), 306–318 (2013)
59. Jones, M.C., Taylor, G.S., Spencer, B.A.: The CEO/CIO relationship revisited: an empirical assessment of satisfaction with IS. Inf. Manage. **29**(3), 123–130 (1995)
60. Kaarst-Brown, M.L.: Understanding an organization's view of the CIO: the role of assumptions about IT. MIS Q. Exec. **4**(2), 287–301 (2005)
61. Karahanna, E., Watson, R.T.: Information systems leadership. IEEE Trans. Eng. Manage. **53**(2), 171–176 (2006)
62. Karimi, J., Gupta, Y.P., Somers, T.M.: The congruence between a firm's competitive strategy and information technology leader's rank and role. J. Manage. Inf. Syst. **13**(1), 63–88 (1996)
63. Kearns, G.S.: The effect of top management support of SISP on strategic IS management: insights from the US electric power industry. Omega. **34**(3), 236–253 (2006)
64. Kearns, G.S., Lederer, A.L.: A resource-based view of strategic IT alignment: how knowledge sharing creates competitive advantage. Decis. Sci. **34**(1), 1–29 (2003)
65. Kearns, G.S., Sabherwal, R.: Strategic alignment between business and information technology: a knowledge-based view of behaviors, outcome, and consequences. J. Manage. Inf. Syst. **23**(3), 129–162 (2006)

66. Keen, P.G.W.: Shaping the Future: Business Design Through Information Technology. Harvard Business School Press, Boston (1991)
67. Kettinger, W.J., Zhang, C., Marchand, D.A.: CIO and business executive leadership approaches to establishing company-wide information orientation. MIS Q. Exec. 10(4), 157–174 (2011)
68. Kurke, L.B., Aldrich, H.E.: Note – Mintzberg was right!: a replication and extension of the nature of managerial work. Manage. Sci. 29(8), 975–984 (2011)
69. Lane, M.S., Koronios, A.: Critical competencies required for the role of the modern CIO. In: Proceedings of the 18th Australasian Conference on Information Systems, paper 90 (2007)
70. Lederer, A.L., Mendelow, A.L.: Information resource planning: overcoming difficulties in identifying top management's objectives. MIS Q. 11(3), 389–399 (1987)
71. Lederer, A.L., Mendelow, A.L.: Convincing top management of the strategic potential of information systems. MIS Q. 12(4), 525–534 (1988)
72. Lee, D.M.S., Trauth, E.M., Farwell, D.: Critical skills and knowledge requirements of IS professionals: a joint academic/industry investigation. MIS Q. 19(3), 313–340 (1995)
73. Leidner, D.E., Mackay, J.M.: How incoming CIOs transition into their new jobs. MIS Q. Exec. 6(1), 17–28 (2007)
74. Leidner, D.E., Beatty, R.C., Mackay, J.M.: How CIOs manage IT during economic decline: surviving and thriving amid uncertainty. MIS Q. Exec. 2(1), 1–14 (2003)
75. Li, D., Ding, F., Wu, J.: Innovative usage of information systems: does CIO role effectiveness matter? In: Proceedings of the Pacific Asia Conference on Information Systems, paper 81 (2012)
76. Li, M., Ye, R.L.: Information technology and firm performance: linking with environmental, strategic and managerial contexts? Inf. Manage. 35(1), 43–51 (1999)
77. Li, Y., Tan, C.-H.: Matching business strategy and CIO characteristics: the impact on organizational performance. J. Bus. Res. 66(2), 248–259 (2013)
78. Li, Y., Tan, C.-H., Teo, H.-H., Tan, B.C.Y.: Innovative usage of information technology in Singapore organizations: do CIO characteristics make a difference? IEEE Trans. Eng. Manage. 53(2), 177–190 (2006)
79. Luftman, J., Brier, T.: Achieving and sustaining business-IT alignment. Calif. Manage. Rev. 42(1), 109–122 (1999)
80. Luftman, J., Kempaiah, R.: An update on business-IT alignment: "A line" has been drawn. MIS Q. Exec. 6(3), 165–177 (2007)
81. Maes, R., De Vries, E.J.: Information leadership: the CIO as orchestrator and equilibrist. In: Proceedings of the 29th International Conference on Information Systems, paper 58 (2008)
82. Martin, E.W.: Critical success factors of chief MIS/DP executives. MIS Q. 6(2), 1–9 (1982)
83. Martinko, M.J., Gardner, W.L.: Structured observation of managerial work: a replication and synthesis. J. Manage. Stud. 27(3), 329–357 (1990)
84. Maruca, R.F.: Are CIOs obsolete? Harv. Bus. Rev. 78(2), 55–61 (2000)
85. Mata, F.J., Fuerst, W.L., Barney, J.B.: Information technology and sustained competitive advantage: a resource-based analysis. MIS Q. 19(4), 487–505 (1995)
86. McKenna, S.: Predispositions and context in the development of managerial skills. J. Manage. Dev. 23(7), 664–677 (2004)
87. Medcof, J.W.: The organizational influence of the chief technology officer. R&D Manage. 38 (4), 406–420 (2008)
88. Mintzberg, H.: Managerial work: analysis from observation. Manage. Sci. 18(2), 97–110 (1971)
89. Mintzberg, H.: The Nature of Managerial Work. Harper & Row, New York (1973)
90. Nelson, K.M., Cooprider, J.G.: The contribution of shared knowledge to IS group performance. MIS Q. 20(4), 409–432 (1996)
91. Paolillo, J.G.P.: Role profiles for managers in different functional areas. Group Org. Manage. 12(1), 109–118 (1987)

92. Pavett, C.M., Lau, A.W.: Managerial work: the influence of hierarchical level and functional specialty. Acad. Manage. J. **26**(1), 170–177 (1983)
93. Peppard, J.: Unlocking the performance of the chief information officer (CIO). Calif. Manage. Rev. **52**(4), 73–99 (2010)
94. Peppard, J., Lambert, R., Edwards, C.: Whose job is it anyway?: organizational information competencies for value creation. Inf. Syst. J. **10**(4), 291–322 (2000)
95. Peppard, J., Edwards, C., Lambert, R.: Clarifying the ambiguous role of the CIO. MIS Q. Exec. **10**(1), 31–44 (2011)
96. Pervan, G.: How chief executive officers in large organizations view the management of their information systems. J. Inf. Technol. **13**(2), 95–109 (1998)
97. Piccoli, G., Ives, B.: IT-dependent strategic initiatives and sustained competitive advantage: a review and synthesis of the literature. MIS Q. **29**(4), 747–776 (2005)
98. Porter, M.E.: Competitive Strategy: Techniques for Analyzing Industries and Competitors. Free Press, New York (1980)
99. Porter, M.E.: What is strategy? Harv. Bus. Rev. **74**(6), 61–78 (1996)
100. Preston, D. S., Karahanna, E.: Mechanisms for the development of shared mental models between the CIO and the top management team. In: Proceedings of the 25th International Conference on Information Systems, paper 37 (2004)
101. Preston, D.S., Karahanna, E.: How to develop a shared vision: the key to IS strategic alignment. MIS Q. Exec. **8**(1), 1–8 (2009)
102. Preston, D.S., Karahanna, E., Rowe, F.: Development of shared understanding between the chief information officer and top management team in U.S. and French organizations: a cross-cultural comparison. IEEE Trans Eng Manage. **53**(2), 191–206 (2006)
103. Preston, D.S., Leidner, D.E., Chen, D.: CIO leadership profiles: implications of matching CIO authority and leadership capability on IT impact. MIS Q. Exec. **7**(2), 57–69 (2008)
104. Raghunathan, B., Raghunathan, T.S.: Relationship of the rank of information systems executive to the organizational role and planning dimensions of information systems. J. Manage. Inf. Syst. **6**(1), 111–126 (1989)
105. Ragu-Nathana, B.S., Apigianb, C.H., Ragu-Nathana, T.S., Tu, Q.: A path analytic study of the effect of top management support for information systems performance. Omega. **32**(6), 459–471 (2004)
106. Ranganathan, C, Jha, S.: Examining the compensation of chief information officers: do firm performance, size and industry membership matter? In: Proceedings of the 11th Americas Conference on Information Systems, paper 363 (2005)
107. Ranganathan, C, Jha, S.: Do CIOs matter? Assessing the value of CIO presence in top management teams. In: Proceedings of the 29th International Conference on Information Systems, paper 56 (2008)
108. Rathnam, R.G., Johnsen, J., Wen, H.J.: Alignment of business strategy and IT strategy: a case study of a Fortune 50 financial services company. J. Comput. Inf. Syst. **45**(2), 1–8 (2004)
109. Rattanasampan, W., Chaidaroon, S.: The applications of communication competence framework for CIOs. In: Proceedings of the 9th Americas Conference on Information Systems, paper 160 (2003)
110. Reich, B.H., Benbasat, I.: Measuring the linkage between business and information technology objectives. MIS Q. **20**(1), 55–81 (1996)
111. Reich, B.H., Benbasat, I.: Factors that influence the social dimension of alignment between business and information technology objectives. MIS Q. **24**(1), 81–113 (2000)
112. Riedl, R., Kobler, M., Roithmayr, F.: Zur personellen Verankerung der IT-Funktion im Vorstand börsennotierter Unternehmen: Ergebnisse einer inhaltsanalytischen Betrachtung. Wirtschaftsinformatik. **50**(2), 111–128 (2008)
113. Rockart, J.F., Ball, L., Bullen, C.V.: Future role of the information systems executive. MIS Q. **6**(4), 1–14 (1982)
114. Rockart, J.F., Earl, M.J., Ross, J.W.: Eight imperatives for the new IT organization. Sloan Manage. Rev. **38**(1), 43–55 (1996)

115. Ross, J.W., Feeny, D.F.: The evolving role of the CIO. In: Zmud, R.W. (ed.) Framing the domains of IT management: projecting the future...through the past (pp. 385–402). Pinnaflex Press, Cincinnati (2000). Also published as CISR working paper No. 308 (August 1999)
116. Ross, J.W., Beath, C.M., Goodhue, D.L.: Develop long-term competitiveness through IT assets. Sloan Manage. Rev. **38**(1), 31–42 (1996)
117. Sambamurthy, V., Zmud, R.W.: Arrangements for information technology governance: a theory of multiple contingencies. MIS Q. **23**(2), 261–290 (1999)
118. Sambamurthy, V., Bharadwaj, A., Grover, V.: Shaping agility through digital options: reconceptualizing the role of information technology in contemporary firms. MIS Q. **27**(2), 237–263 (2003)
119. Sharma, S., Rai, A.: An assessment of the relationship between ISD leadership characteristics and IS innovation adoption in organizations. Inf. Manage. **40**(5), 391–401 (2003)
120. Smaltz, D.H., Sambamurthy, V., Agarwal, R.: The antecedents of CIO role effectiveness in organizations: an empirical study in the healthcare sector. IEEE Trans. Eng. Manage. **53**(2), 207–222 (2006)
121. Smith, R.D.: The chief technology officer: strategic responsibilities and relationships. Res. Technol. Manage. **46**(4), 28–36 (2003)
122. Sobol, M.G., Klein, G.: Relation of CIO background, IT infrastructure, and economic performance. Inf. Manage. **46**(5), 271–278 (2009)
123. Spitze, J.M., Lee, J.J.: The renaissance CIO project: the invisible factors of extraordinary success. Calif. Manage. Rev. **54**(2), 72–91 (2012)
124. Stephens, C.S., Ledbetter, W.N., Mitra, A., Ford, F.N.: Executive or functional manager? The nature of the CIO's job. MIS Q. **16**(4), 449–467 (1992)
125. Štemberger, M.I., Manfreda, A., Kovačič, A.: Achieving top management support with business knowledge and role of IT/IS personnel. Int. J. Inf. Manage. **31**(5), 428–436 (2011)
126. Synnott, W.R., Gruber, W.H.: Information Resource Management: Opportunities and Strategies for the 1980s. Wiley, New York (1981)
127. Tallon, P.P.: A process-oriented perspective on the alignment of information technology and business strategy. J. Manage. Inf. Syst. **24**(3), 227–268 (2007)
128. Tan, F.B., Gallupe, R.B.: Aligning business and information systems thinking: a cognitive approach. IEEE Trans. Eng. Manage. **53**(2), 223–237 (2006)
129. Thoits, P.A.: Identity structures and psychological well-being: gender and marital status comparisons. Soc. Psychol. Q. **55**(3), 236–256 (1992)
130. Tubre, T.C., Collins, J.M.: Jackson and Schuler (1985) revisited: a meta-analysis of the relationships between role ambiguity, role conflict, and job performance. J. Manage. **26**(1), 155–169 (2000)
131. Venkatesh, V., Brown, S.A., Bala, H.: Bridging the qualitative-quantitative divide: guidelines for conducting mixed methods research in information systems. MIS Q. **37**(1), 21–54 (2013)
132. Watson, R.T.: Influences on the IS manager's perceptions of key issues: information scanning and the relationship with the CEO. MIS Q. **14**(2), 217–231 (1990)
133. Watson, R.T., Kelly, G.G., Galliers, R.D., Brancheau, J.C.: Key issues in information systems management: an international perspective. J. Manage. Inf. Syst. **13**(4), 91–117 (1997)
134. Watts, S., Henderson, J.C.: Innovative IT climates: CIO perspectives. J. Strateg. Inf. Syst. **15**(2), 125–151 (2006)
135. Webster, J., Watson, R.T.: Analyzing the past to prepare for the future: writing a literature review. MIS Q. **26**(2), xiii–xxiii (2002)
136. Weill, P.: Don't just lead, govern: how top-performing firms govern IT. MIS Q. Exec. **3**(1), 1–17 (2004)
137. Weill, P., Broadbent, M.: Leveraging the New Infrastructure: How Market Leaders Capitalize on Information Technology. Harvard Business School Press, Boston (1998)
138. Weill, P., Ross, J.W.: IT Governance: How Top Performers Manage IT Decision Rights for Superior Performance. Harvard Business School Press, Boston (2004)

139. Weill, P., Woerner, S.L.: The future of the CIO in a digital economy. MIS Q. Exec. **12**(2), 65–75 (2013)
140. Welbourne, T.M., Johnson, D.E., Erez, A.: The role-based performance scale: validity analysis of a theory-based measure. Acad. Manage. J. **41**(5), 540–555 (1998)
141. Willson, P., Pollard, C.: Exploring IT governance in theory and practice in a large multi-national organisation in Australia. Inf. Syst. Manage. **26**(2), 98–109 (2009)
142. Wu, J.-H., Chen, Y.-C., Lin, H.-H.: Developing a set of management needs for IS managers: a study of necessary managerial activities and skills. Inf. Manage. **41**(4), 413–429 (2004)
143. Yayla, A.A., Hu, Q.: The effect of board of directors' IT awareness on CIO compensation and firm performance. Decis. Sci. **45**(3), 401–436 (2014)
144. Zhang, H., Gao, T.: An empirical research on the status and role of listed companies' CFO in corporate governance. Can. Soc. Sci. **6**(2), 93–98 (2006)

Printed in the United States ...

By Bo... ...

Printed in the United States
By Bookmasters